PEEPS
:: at the ::
MIGHTY.

ARNOLD BENNETT.

: PEEPS :
AT
THE MIGHTY

By

PATRICK BRAYBROOKE. F.R.S.L.

Essay Index Reprint Series

BOOKS FOR LIBRARIES PRESS, INC.
FREEPORT, NEW YORK

[1966]

FIRST PUBLISHED 1927
REPRINTED 1966

G.L.

Printed In The United States of America

AUTHOR'S NOTE.

I have always held it as a firm opinion that an Essay is a most elastic form of literary art. With this in mind, no apology is necessary for a book that treats of subjects as far apart as Dean Inge on Cardinal Newman and Mr. Leacock writing about England.

can only hope that old friends may be interested in this volume of " gossip " and that I may gain a few new friends.

PATRICK BRAYBROOKE. F.R.S.L.

Leinster Square,
        Hyde Park.

Spring, 1927.

DEDICATION.

TO MY FATHER AND MOTHER.

CONTENTS.

Peep Number One.

H. G. WELLS AND A LUNATIC.

IT is not very long since Mr. Wells published a book which he called ' Christina Alberta's Father." Now there are a good many people who always imagine that Mr. Wells is somewhere near to the top of the stars or somewhere not too far out of the suburbs. In " Christina Alberta's Father " Mr. Wells studies a phenomenon that can be found in any suburb and I imagine that it might be found in any star.

The phenomenon is of course lunacy and it gives Mr. Wells something to be quite angry about and it gives him equal scope to be more sympathetic than usual.

At the very moment that I find myself writing this Essay, one of the great London newspapers has been indulging in a kind of harmless stunt which has discussed what might happen if Christ came to London. The discussion has been contirbuted to by bishops at the one end and various noted authors at the other. The result of the discussion seems to have been an opinion that Christ, if He came to London would find the City

9

not so bad as some of our moralists would imagine.
But no one seems to have seen that if Christ did
come to London nothing would happen for the
very excellent reason that the police would remove
such a dangerous person to the nearest lunatic
asylum, for the police have no imagination, if
they had they would probably not be policemen
at all.

Mr. Wells goes back much farther than Christ,
he gets back to the beginnings of history and he
seems to say to himself that there was a very
great king and his name was Sargon. Now it
would make quite a good story to imagine that
a respectable laundryman had a sudden idea
that he was Sargon and that it was his duty so
to inform a waiting world. At the same time
such a story besides being a good tale would give
Mr. Wells a chance to say something about our
tyrannical lunatics who look after our lunatics.
So Sargon is a benefactor to us, for he, by taking
possession of Mr. Preemby lets us know what Mr.
Wells thinks about lunacy and there is nothing
under the sun that needs so much talking about.
For in this land of England we treat our lunatics
with mere bare consideration, the public which
is even less imaginative than the police, still laughs
at madness, but then the average Englishman
cannot help laughing at lunacy for he imagines
that of all the nations in the world, he is the
member of the only sane one.

Mr. Wells writes of what would happen if a
laundryman came to London and announced that

he was Sargon, King of Kings. It will be interesting to see what Mr. Wells thinks would happen.

.   .   .   .

Soon after Mr. Preemby is possessed of the
idea that he is Sargon we are introduced to a
clever discussion as to whether a man is insane
who thinks he is a king. Of course the lunatic
asylums are full of " kings " but does Mr. Wells
think they ought to be there ? This is what he
writes :—

" Let's hope that lasts. I don't see that
a man is insane because he believes he is a
King or an Emperor—if someone tells him
he is. After all, George the Fifth has no
other grounds for imagining he is a King."

But this is precisely where Mr. Wells goes most
delightfully wrong. The man in a lunatic asylum
is not put there because he thinks he is a king
but because the thought will quite likely evolve
into something that will be uncomfortable for
the reigning monarch. Again, when Mr. Wells
writes that George the Fifth has no grounds for
being a king beyond the fact that many people
have told him that he is, he is again writing
something foolish. Mr. Wells has only to study
the descent of kings to see that George the Fifth
has more than a mere number of imaginings to
warrant his position on the English throne.

Nobody cares a tinker's cuss if a bank clerk
in Kensal Green has an idea that he is the King of
England. As long as he keeps this good news

within the bounds of his small villa all is well, if he likes he can " rule " the subjects in his villa. But as soon as the Kensal Green bank clerk thinks that he ought to leave his Kensal Green villa and move to Buckingham Palace, then it comes that he is rapidly removed to Hanwell.

So Mr. Wells rambles on.

" Fancying yourself a King isn't lunacy and behaving in accordance with that idea isn't lunacy either."

Surely this is the reverse of what is true. The man who magines he is a king is absolutely insane because the sane man would know perfectly well that if he was a king and had not been dethroned he would have no need to assert that he was a king. But the man who thinks he is a king has to continually insist that he is a king, that he is the Ruler of the People, that deference should be paid to him. Mr. Wells would be most unwise to allow himself to be ruled by one of those people who think that they are in reality king, he would find that the " sanity " of these good people was probably, to say the least of it, a little tyrannical.

In the course of his wanderings, Mr. Preemby tries to get into Buckingham Palace and this gives Mr. Wells a chance to write what a policeman really does think about the maniac who attempts to gain access to the king. I rather think that Mr. Wells thinks the police are a little unsympathetic but after all getting a madman away from the Palace is but one of the many duties for which a grateful State pays them money. The policeman has met Sargon and is not impressed but why should he be when he has just seen the Almighty driven away in a taxi cab !

" The policeman at the gate to whom they addressed themselves listened gravely to their inquiries, making no instant reply. He belonged to that great majority of English speakers who are engaged upon the improvement of the word ' yes.' His particular idea was to make it long and purry."

The policeman on duty outside the palace is a machine, there can be no exceptions, no manner of man must be allowed to see the king.

" There is no exceptions," I says. " Not even if you was a close relation. We get no options here. We're just machines."

Then Sargon demands that it is the duty of a king to see those who desire to see him. Perhaps Mr. Wells is a little on the side of poor Mr. Preemby, for the stolid policeman answers :

" I says, very likely it is sir. But we policemen aren't in any position to 'elp it," I says, " much less alter it."

And it is all in the day's work, if Sargon does come up to Buckingham Palace, the policeman will be so little impressed that he will not remember which way the great potentate went.

" ' It might be Piccadilly way,' said the policeman, ' it might be down towards Trafalgar Square. Fact is, sir, I didn't notice.' "

The policemen are machines but now and then

they are quite human and more human than is sometimes suspected. So far poor Mr. Preemby makes less impression on the world as the mighty Sargon than he did as the laundryman. Mr. Wells knows only too fully that great potentates cannot impress the stolid citizens of London, it takes a great film favourite to do that.

. . . .

With a good deal of cunning, Mr. Wells gives a picture of the inner feelings of poor Mr. Preemby after his startling transformation from a mere commonplace laundryman to being Sargon, King of Kings. It is like this ; wonderfully good insight, not a bit exaggerated.

" It is no doubt a very wonderful and glorious thing to discover that instead of being the rather obscure widower of a laundry proprietor with no particular purpose in the world one is Lord of the Whole World, but it is also, to a conscientious man anxious to do right, an extremely disturbing and oppressive discovery."

And this was his mission. It is really quite pathetic, for no one is so pathetic as a missioner, for how can you teach a people which only cares for money and dresses its every woman as a professional prostitute ? Yet Mr. Preemby has his ideal, as Sargon, London will listen, the great city that swarms with human ants and human snakes, human angels and inhuman devils, these shall listen to the glorious message of Sargon, alias Mr. Preemby. I think Mr. Wells is a little

sorry for Sargon, to plant him in the midst of this
twentieth century whirlpool of chaos.

"And he had come back to heal the swarming
world's disorders and reinstate the deep peace of
old Sumeria once again."

After all there is no reason why Sargon should
not start his world mission from a Bloonsbury
boarding house. In any case it gives Mr. Wells a
chance to show what the common or garden
English person thinks of lunatics. This is how the
advent of the King of Kings struck the boarding
house. But even if Mr. Preemby had been Sargon,
it would take the average Bloomsbury boarding
house intelligence sometime to get used to it.

"I've let the second floor to a lunatic, said
Bobby breaking the news to his ground floor
friends Mr. and Mrs. Malmesbury."

"Oh, Bobby! and with Susan about! cried
Mrs. Malmesbury reproachfully."

Again a little further on in the peculiar career
of Sargon, Mr. Wells shows us how the idea is
revolving and evolving in the mind of Mr.
Preemby. There is a conception of greatness but
Sargon cannot all at once throw off the Preemby
influence. Perhaps most lunatics of the megalo-
mania kind oscillate between their " greatness "
and their poor miserable selves, perhaps they are
never quite convinced.

"Yet even when Sargon doubted he believed.
It is a very comprehensible paradox. He knew
clearly that to be Sargon was to be real, was to
signify and make all the world signify was to go

back into the past and reach right out into the future, was to escape altogether from the shrivelled insignficance of the Preemby life. To be Sargon was to achieve not only greatness but goodness, Sargon could give and Sargon could dare. Sargon could face lions and die for his people, but Preemby could go round three fields, had been known to go round three fields to evade the hostility of a barking terrier. Preemby's world was dust and dirt, a mud speck in infinite space and there was no life on it but abjection ; Sargon was rebirth into a world of spacious things."

We have, I suggest here, a very true picture of the dual mind of a lunatic. Mr. Wells makes it quite clear that, as Sargon, Mr. Preemby is an idealist. He makes it equally clear that as Sargon Mr. Preemby can satisfy an ambition to be something. The interesting problem then is, which does Mr. Wells think is paramount in the Sargon idea of Mr. Preemby, a wish to make the world better, to restore Sumeria, or the personal ambition of a laundryman to be a great potentate ?

It is I think quite obvious that in Mr. Well's mind, Sargon puts his idealism first, his wish that he shall restore a kingdom.

We see him on the steps of Saint Paul's Cathedral, those steps from which all the nations of the world at sometime gaze down on the great city that is London.

" It was with an extraordinary sense of power over men's destinies that he stood now upon Saint Paul's steps and reflected that even now men and women might be passing by, among these busy men thronging the pavement, among the people in omnibuses, among the girls clattering away at their typewriters, behind the upstairs windows, over whose busy pretty, undistinguished lives hung the challenge of his summons."

A mighty prospect indeed and a prospect that can but lead to a bed in a lunatic asylum. Such is the weary and depressing road along which we follow Mr. Preemby but we would not miss the journey, for by undertaking it, we are enabled to know what Mr. Wells really does think about the hateful treatment of the insane.

There is no need to travel all the miserable journey which Sargon undertakes, as he attempts to convince an unsympathetic world that he is indeed a great potentate. There is no need to recount the miserable episode when Mr. Preemby is hurled out of a restaurant. No ; we will proceed further to the day when Mr. Preemby is examined by a doctor and sent off to a mental " hospital." The doctor is admirably drawn, like most hospital doctors he is moderately pleasant and interested in the new " case." For a patient is only a case to a doctor, he is not a human being, he is a case, if he gets well it will be dull, if he dies, well they may find sonething of interest in the delightful official post mortem, those barbarities which are sandwiched in between the ministry of healing that goes on in the wards a few walls away.

The dialogue is delightful, it is true, it is exquisite.

"Well ? " said the man in the grey suit.

"My name is Sargon. I do not know why I have been brought here. Is this a hospital? I understand it is. I am not ill.

"You may be ill without knowing it.

"No."

"We just want to have you here for a bit to have a look at you."

After this farcical interview, Sargon is handed over to some kind of hospital attendant and having no wish to be sent into a ward, we get a little glimpse of the tenderness and courtesy of our hospitals. Mr. Wells shows the attendant up in his true light, an odious bully. Mr. Preemby has suggested that he has no wish to proceed further, it is too much for the dignity of Sargon. And it is too much for the hospital official.

"No," he said, "I do not want to go further into this place. I do not wish it. Let me return. I have disciples to call and many things to do."

The full moon of Jordan's face displayed incredulous astonishment that passed into fierceness. 'Wot ? ' he said."

"He left a tremendous pause after ' Wot ' and then spoke very rapidly. ' None of your tricks 'ere, you thundering old bastard.' With a swift movement his huge, raw, red hand gripped Sargon by the upper arm. He thin lips were retracted to show his teeth ; his eyes seemed popping out. He gripped not to hold but to pinch and compress and injure and he dug fingers in between muscle and bone, so that Sargon stared at him with dilated eyes and uttered a sharp involuntary cry of pain."

Once in the observation ward, things were no better. Mr. Wells remarks that Sargon was passed from hand to hand as if he was but a parcel. This is exactly what does happen. A patient in a hospital is treated as a piece of dirt, if he shows the least sign of any mental derangement.

" Impelled partly by the arm of Mr. Higgs and partly by his natural disposition to please, Sargon got into bed. Mr. Higgs assisted him in a rough brotherly fashion. But before Sargon could pull up the clothes about him Mr. Higgs, glancing over his shoulder, became aware of something that was happening down the room—Sargon could not see what."

In an instant the genial authoritativeness of Mr. Higgs gave way to rage. ' Yaaps, you dirty old devil,' said Mr. Higgs, ' Your're at it again ! He quitted Sargon and ran down the room very swiftly. Sargon sat up in bed to see what was happening. Three or four of the other patients did the same. A very dirty old man with a face of extreme misery, who was sitting in a chair, was seized upon and bumped down and up and hit several times with great vigour by Mr. Higgs."

That is the reward of the insane in this Christian country of England, this Christian country that has reduced Christianity to a form of social convenience. The reward of the insane is that they are herded together like filthy swine, they are " cared for " by low type attendants and third rate women, they are struck repeatedly, they are put in a building that looks more deadly than a prison and they are under a kind of God who is the medical superintendant and he has probably enough intelligence not to be turned out of his job. Meanwhile the outside world cares not one jot, it is left to those who drive a pen to draw attention to these things. The Church says nothing, she preaches how Christ has changed the world, but she does not demand that our lunatics shall be better looked after.

.   .   .   .

One somewhat long quotation fron Mr. Wells will give exactly what he does feel about the condition of those who are charged with insanity. It is a good word " charged," for the insane man or woman are treated as criminals, with this one difference that they are treated far more savagely, and their " crime" has been the unfortunate fact that medicine at present cannot prevent insanity, it seems pretty clear that it cannot treat it with paramount success.

I do not believe that Mr. Wells in the least exaggerates the case, possibly he underestimates it.

" And while Sargon was being steered back to bed, firmly rather than gently, in the grip of Jordan, the justice and the doctor filled in and signed the forms that were necessary to deprive him of nearly every right he possessed as a human being. For there is no trial by jury and no writ of habeas-corpus in Britain for the unfortunate charged with insanity. He may not plead in public and there is no one to whom he may appeal. He may write complaints but they will be neglected ; his most urgent expostulations will be disregarded in favour of any dull attendant's asseverations. He is handed over to the nearly autocratic control of under educated, ill paid, ill fed and overworked attendants. Every night and every day seems endless to him at first and then the nights and days fall into a sort of routine and become unimportant and pass away more and more rapidly. He is almost always kept in a state of bodily discomfort, always rather ill from the ill prepared and sometimes tainted food, and much incommoded by the clumsy drugging and particularly by the administration of violent purgatives. In croton oil alone are our asylums truly generous. He has excellent reason for fearing many of his fellow inmates and for a servile obedience to the attendants in charge of him. A medical superintendent hovers in the back ground ; a medical staff with no special training in mental science. They pass through the wards at the appointed times, avoiding trouble, seeing as little as possible."

This is of course a very scathing indictment. And the saddest part of the whole thing is that Mr. Wells admits that he can see no remedy. For he writes : " And, after all, what can they do ? "

If nothing can be done then it merely shows that the English with their love of liberty and fairplay, their boast of being the one nation to lead the world, if nothing can be done, then the English are a nation of detestable hypocrites. But something can be done. In the first place a better class of attendents could be secured. Second, a better feeling about insane people could be fostered. Most people are ashamed of being connected with anyone who is insane, get rid of them, they contaminate, they are a drag, get them away, shut them up behind high walls, let them curse man and curse God there, let them practice all their detestable and deplorable habits out of the sight of sane men. Get rid of the insane member of the family, punish him for his crime, make him suffer every imaginable torture of mind, but be very careful that he is no trouble to us. That is the attitude. I believe it were better that the hopelessly insane were put painlessly to death that they that should be incarcerated in these diabolical traps which pose as mental hospitals.

The medical superintendents are well paid, they do not wish that there shall be no insane, for if there were no insane, there would be no asylums and there would be no fat salaries.

But to return to Mr. Wells, Sargon has failed in his mission more miserably than he could even have dreamed of. His end is mere humble death and perhaps it is the best end. For had he lived, it seems that his fate would have been an asylum. His end is simple and Mr. Wells writes of it quietly and with dignity.

" But Sargon did not live forty years more,

nor thirty, nor twenty. He lived just a day under seven weeks from that conversation. It was a clear November night with frost in the air. The nurse heard him cough and rushed out to him. He was looking at Sirius through Lambon's field-glasses and she had to drag him in by main force. She lost her temper; there was an ungracious struggle."

But it was poor Sargon's last fight for: " The next day he was in no state to leave his bed. Yet he tossed about and exposed his inflamed chest in feeble attempts to read. ' I know nothing,' he complained. For a while he got better again, and then it is highly probable that he went to his open window in the night and sat for a long time wondering at the stars. After that came a relapse and a week or so of struggle, and then after a phase of delirium came great weakness, and then one night, death. He was quite alone when he died."

· · · · · · ·

Whichever way you choose to look at this story of Mr. Preemby, alias Sargon King of Kings, the atmosphere is tragic. Lunacy of any kind is always the most dreadful tragedy. It is tragic because it is hopeless, there is no help for the mentally afflicted, no one understands them, they stray but have no shepherd, they are shunned by man, they live in the world but the world is to them but a bitter place full of dark misery. They can only hope for death and even then have no assurance that it will lead to anything better. And if it was that Mr. Preemby was not insane, even if he had been really a reincarnation of Sargon, the theme is still tragic. For Sargon, King of Kings is rejected and Mr. Wells has penned the story of a failure.

I am quite aware that I have dealt with only one side of Mr. Well's " Christina Alberta's Father." But I wished in this short Essay to examine something of what Mr. Wells thought of our asylums. As I have said earlier, I think that his attack is unfair in only one respect, that is that it is not severe enough.

Had I been able I should like to have written also of the absolutely delightful study of Mr. Preemby's daughter and her evolution from a detestable modern woman to a woman with some semblance of humanity.

It is all done in the best Wells genius. More need not be said.

As a character, Mr. Preemby is of course a person who excites sympathy and a certain amount of respect. For I believe primarily, that Mr. Wells would have us to believe that Mr. Preemby wished to be Sargon that he might improve conditions for the rest of the world. His reward from a grateful State is of course incarceration in a lunatic asylum.

Mr. Wells writes in this book with almost a terrifying realism and there is a breath of anger in all he says. Officialism is condemned and rightly, for officialism is the work of Satan executed by miserable little petty officials

In Mr. Well's book there is a subtle warning. Remain as you are. If you are a laundryman, do not aspire to be a great potentate. For if this greatness is thrust upon you, you will most assuredly follow the great Sargon and be hurled into the very internals of a ghastly lunatic asylum.

END OF PEEP ONE.

DEAN INGE & CARDINAL NEWMAN.

SOMETIMES, during the hot evenings the comparative silence of the London square in which I live is broken by the sound of a very old man singing a very old hymn. The sound of the hymn first stirs away in the distance, then it grows louder and louder, the sound passes my window, and then gradually it fades away and all is at as it was before the melody broke the silences which collect in parts of London. The old man who sings, sings one of the most beautiful hymns in the English language, and the hymn I refer to is " Lead, Kindly Light," by Cardinal Newman.

The singing of the old man set me reading again the marvellous Essay on Newman which Dean Inge wrote in his " Outspoken Essays." I very much doubt if a better appreciation of the Cardinal has ever been written.

In this Essay I propose to deal with a few of the considerations that Dean Inge makes about this Cardinal, this curious ascetic figure that flashed across the Victorian era, a figure that stills interests and perplexes, still calls forth unbounded enthusiasm or intense dislike.

There are certain Roman Catholic Apologists who have an intense dislike of Dean Inge, in fact they carry their dislike so far that they have no hesitation in saying that the Dean cannot argue like a gentleman, which means of course that he is far too clever for them. Now, there has always been a certain type of thought which has proclaimed that Cardinal Newman was extremely happy in the Catholic Church and I have no intention of saying that I believe this necessarily to be mere propaganda about a notable convert.

What has to be examined in this part of my Essay is what Dean Inge says about this alleged happiness of Newman when he left the Anglican Communion and attached himself to the Roman Church.

Dean Inge has no hesitation whatever in saying that Newman in the Catholic Church found nothing but wordly failure. This is not of course the same thing as saying that he was unhappy. But Dean Inge writes of his failure in no half-hearted manner.

" Moreover, his record as a Roman ecclesiastic is one of almost unrelieved failure. If he had died eighteen years after his secession when he had already looked upon himself as an old man whose course was nearly run, he would have been regarded as one who had sacrificed a great career in the Church of England for neglect and obscurity."

But he did not die and although generally

speaking, Newman was a failure from the point
of view of many abortive schemes, he died a
Cardinal and in the eyes of the world the Vatican
did not leave him entirely alone without recognition. But even the Cardinal's hat was something
that really had to be given, according to Dean
Inge. He sums up the unpleasant position concisely and fairly.

" When Manning, Archdeacon of Chichester,
followed his example and joined the Roman
Church, Newman was confronted with a still
more subtle and relentless opponent, whose
hostility was never relaxed till the accession of a
Liberal Pope made it no longer possible to resist
the bestowal of tardy honours upon a feeble
octogenarian. The recognition came in time to
soothe his decline, but too late to enable him to
leave his mark upon the administration of the
Roman Church."

Perhaps it may be summed up that the honour
was an " unwilling honour " and perhaps Newman
would have been a greater man if he had refused
it. But those who can refuse honours, even those
given almost reluctantly, are so far and few
between, that their names might be counted.

It will be quite convenient at this moment to
examine the very controversial question as to
whether, at one time in his life, Newman intended
returning to the Anglican communion.

At any rate for Dean Inge, there was in Newman
" a wistful yearning after the friends and the
Church he had left." But it could not have been

really serious, for as Dean Inge points out, to leave the Church of Rome is a fall in pride so enormous that it can scarcely be contemplated. But the question of Newman's yearning (and his whole life has ever seemed a journey of wistfulness), allows Dean Inge to make a very wise comment upon something that may be called the patronising attitude of Rome to the Protestants. This is what the Dean writes on this difficult and provoking question.

" But a man must have vanquished pride in its most insidious form before he can leave the Church of Rome for any other. The aristocratic hauteur of the civis Romanus among barbarians lives on in the sentiment of the Roman Catholic towards Protestants. When Newman was publicly charged with intending to return to Anglicanism, this spirit broke out in a disagreeable and insulting manner."

The result of this charge was of course the unfortunate attack on Newman by Kingsley. For once Kingsley allowed anger to defeat his judgment and his violent attack on Newman, as Inge points out, gave Newman a chance to gain a more favourable hearing in England.

There is no need to go into the frenzied discussion, the appalling spectacle of a bitter battle between two great Divines, there is no need for more than bitter melancholy that such a struggle between Kingsely and Newman, is but the prototype of the perpetual bitter battle between the Catholics and the Protestants.

The immediate result of the bitter controversy between Kingsley and Newman was
of course the "Apologia" which Dean Inge
admits was "a powerful defence of Catholicism."

I have already said that Dean Inge writes with
the utmost frankness that the life of Newman in
the Catholic Church was a failure. Very well,
then the problem is, why is it that the life of the
curious lonely ascetic Cardinal still interests, still
stirs the emotions, still calls to us from the far
off days of the old Tractarians, still intrigues the
busy twentieth century ?

I must let Dean Inge discuss the problem.

He at once says that the interest is mainly
personal and psychological. But I think it may
also be that Newman is a symbol. He is a symbol
of what the Roman Church really is. Newman
is on the one hand, intensely ambitious, on the
other he is extremely unwordly, his shadowed
appearance at Oxford is a photograph of his soul.
It may be that the Roman Church is something
the same, those who are not of her communion
have ever been amazed at her dualism. Her
incredible ambitions on the one hand, her amazing
unwordliness on the other. Men have seen her
diabolical cruelty and her Divine kindness, in
Newman they see something of the same. They
see Newman imbued with that devilry which is
known as theological cruelty when he attacks
Kingsley, they see Newman tender and full of
understanding in "Lead, Kindly Light," and the
glorious idea of the angel's faces, which though

" lost awhile," still smile. In Newman they see this terrific dualism and this terrific dualism also exists in that Church into which Newman made his irrevocable " step."

Here is a brilliant picture of the young Newman, in the days of his boyhood, when he dreams, when he begins to see that he will one day be a man, that one day he will be a priest.

" He has left us, in the 'Apologia,' a picture of his precocious and dreamy boyhood, when he lived in a world of his own, peopled by angels and spirits, a world in which the supernatural was the only nature. He was lonely and reserved then as always. It is not for nothing that in his sermons he expatiates so often on the impenetrability of the human soul."

The mental attitude of Newman was again something complex and almost contradictory. He is almost a mystic, that is, he wishes to absorb himself into God, at the same time he is afraid of God. So Dean Inge says that when he was wavering between the Church of England and the Church of Rome, he was pondering over the intensely pragmatic question, " Where shall I be most safe ? " There is something almost petty in this side of Newman's nature, something selfish, something unfathomable.

There is little doubt whatever that Dean Inge is quite certain that the reason Newman left the Anglican Church was because he felt the need of a Divine Society and it could only seem to exist in the Roman Communion.

In this way.

" But the national Church of England was not constituted to resist the national will, and the attempt to reorganise it on Catholic lines was foredoomed to failure."

So the way to Rome was clear, St, Peter's beckoned, and the Oxford towers receded into the far distance.

· Though only in the nature of a suggestion, Inge does mention the possibility that had his party in the English Church been victorious, Newman might have stayed. There is no answer to the problem except the answer from the Catholic side, that he must have come over, but even this dogmatism proves nothing.

But in any case it was probably as well for the Church of England that Newman did go over to Rome, for the very good reason that this extra-ordinary Cardinal was incapable of being a successful leader of any party. Very probably a good deal of his failure in the Roman Church was due to Newman's inability to work pleasantly with other people.

And yet with all, Dean Inge is pretty certain that the Roman Church was wise is not using Newman and not even using him as a tool. The Dean then says a very wise thing again and it is quite surprising how very seldom it is that the Dean of St. Paul's ever says anything that is not wise.

" If the Roman Church would not use him as a tool, it was probably because he would not have been a good tool.   There are some mistakes which that Church seldom makes ; it knows how to choose its men."

And it might be added that the Church of England makes the mistake pretty frequently of putting her men in the wrong place.   Not so the Roman Church but if you are out to conquer nothing less than the entire world, your men need to be most carefully manoeuvred.

Another reason why Newman failed in the Roman Church according to Dean Inge, is that he was possessed of something that might be called half-Catholicism.   It is perhaps yet another reason why modern people are still so fascinated by this strange Cardinal.   He appeared to be in almost every thing half and half ; I have already referred to his mysticism and his fear of God.

" Newman, then, was only half a Catholic. He accepted with all the fervour of a neophyte the principle of submission to Holy Church."

This seems all right so far, why should Rome distrust Newman ?   The answer is fairly simple. The Roman Church demands much more than a general submission to her views and doctrines, she demands a submission to every doctrine and view that she formulates.   Cardinal Newman, as Dean Inge points out, only made a half or general submission to the Roman Church.

" But in place of the official intellectualist apologetic, which an Englishman may study to great advantage in the remarkably able series of manuals issued by the Jesuits of Stonyhurst, he substituted a philosophy of experience which is certainly not Catholic."

In other words, Newman refused to lay on one side all his original reasoning powers and become the absolute slave of a certain religious system. For say what you like, for good or for bad, the Roman Catholic is a slave and very likely it is such an excellent form of slavery that it is good for the individual. But it did not suit Newman and therefore Rome distrusted the ardent convert who hurried out of Littlemore and then hurried into Rome, at times to wish he had not hurried out of the peace of that little near to Oxford village for the whirlpool of wordliness and unworldliness that is the Church of Rome.

The question then of the worldliness of the Roman Church at her worst and the magnificent unselfishness of her saints at her best, calls for a consideration of the question of the attraction of that Church for what Dean Inge calls the average person. I have pointed out that Newman could apparently only find the type of Divine Society he wanted in the Roman Communion.

" To the historian, there is no great mystery about the growth and success of the Western Catholic Church. Christianity was already a syncretistic religion in the second century. Like the other forms of worship with which it competed for the popular favour, it contained the necessary elements of mystery of ethical rule, of social brotherhood and of personal devotion."

So much then for the growth of the great

Western Church. Now for its "attractiveness" to the ordinary person. Dean Inge says in effect that the Roman Church can meet the average needs of the average man. Also :

"It surrounds itself with an impenetrable armour by persuading its adherents that all moral and intellectual scruples, in matters where Holy Church has pronounced its verdict, are suggestions of the Evil One, to be spurned like the prickings of sensuality."

Then there is the appeal to history, and no Church has wrapped up its history so attractively as the Roman Church. Her campaign by means of pamphlets, which often only give one side, is engineered by genius, not unmixed with cunning. Again the strange dualism of inhuman cruelty and supernatural selflessness calls forth the wonder of millions who are ever fascinated by an organisation of which it can never be certain whether it will be cruel or kind.

"Further, Catholicism encourages and blesses that *esprit de corps* which has produced the brightest triumphs of self abnegation as well as the darkest crimes of cruel bigotry in human history."

But to return to Cardinal Newman. Dean Inge would prophesy that the Catholicism of the future will be that of Manning rather than that of Newman If Newman was only a half Catholic in the sense that he repudiated the Church's intellectual position and substituted his own experience, the prophecy seems only too logical. And Dean Inge seems to prove his logic quite satisfactorily and Newman is given the " go by."

"But the Roman Catholicism which has a future is probably that of Manning and not that of Newman. A Church which depends for its strength and prestige on the iron discipline of a central autocracy, and on the fanatical devotion of soldiers who know no duty except obedience, no cause except the interests of their society, can make no terms with disintegrating nominalism, the uncertain subjectivism, of a mind like Newman's."

Dean Inge says that Newman nearly drove a wedge into the solid block that is Catholicism. For in Newman Dean Inge finds a good deal of what we now so loosely call Modernism. The mind of Newman was a revolt and in the Roman Church there can be no revolt, except it can be germinated *from* the Vatican.

The Roman Church can have no dealings with Modernism, it cannot play with the doctrines as does the Church of England. It has been often levelled against the Roman Church that she is tyrannically hostile to any form of Modernism.

In a most brilliant passage which I shall quote at length, Dean Inge gives the reason why the Vatican cannot for its very position be otherwise than adamant against the Modernists. The Vatican must thunder against the thunders of the Modernists for the Church is at stake, those who attempt to thrust Modernism into the Vatican must be thrust out, for the Vatican cannot let those in, who would, if they were successful, alter the essential nature of Holy Church.

" Some rather shallow thinkers in this country have expressed their surprise and regret that the Vatican has refused to make any terms with Modernism. They have supposed that the fault lies with an ignorant and reactionary Pope."

But as Dean Inge writes, this is a perfectly fallacious assumption. He now goes on to say why Modernism cannot to tolerated at the Vatican. It is a scathing indictment of the " shallow thinkers."

" In the first place, Modernism destroys the historical basis of Christianity and converts the Incarnation and Atonement into myths like those of other dying and rising saviour gods which hardly pretend to be historical."

Thus the " uniqueness " of Christianity goes and Rome is the head of a unique Church.

" In the place of the historical God-Man, Modernism gives us the history of the Church as an object of reverence. We are bidden to contemplate an institution of amazingly tough vitality but great adaptability which in its determination to survive has a not only changed colour like a chameleon but has from time to time put forth and discovered new weapons of offence and defence."

Thus we seem to lose the *natural* Divinity of the Church, she becomes something wonderful but not in the strictest sense Holy. Her survival is not a mark that she is Divine but rather that she is amazingly tough. Again from the point of view of philosophy, the Church can have no dealing with Modernism.

" Further, the religious philosophy of Modernism is bad, much worse than the scholasticism it derides. It is in essentials a revival of the sophistry of Protagoras. And if it were metaphysically more respectable than it is, it is so widely opposed to the whole system of Catholic apologetics that if it were accepted it would necessitate a complete reconstruction of Catholic dogma."

So we get back to Newman. And the Catholicism of that Cardinal is not much good for the Church.

" The subjectivism of Newman and the Modernists is fatal to that exclusiveness which is the corner-stone of Catholic policy."

But the great point of importance is that though Dean Inge does not designate Newman as an actual Modernist, he was a dangerous man for the Church of Rome.

" Our conclusion then is that although Newman was not a Modernist, but an exceedingly stiff conservative, he did introduce into the Roman Church a very dangerous and essentially alien habit of thought which has since developed into Modernism. Perhaps Monsignor Talbot was not far wrong, from his own point of view, when he called him ' the most dangerous man in England.' One side of his religion was based on principles which, when logically drawn out, must lead away from Catholicism in the direction of an individualistic religion of experience which makes all truth relative and all values fluid."

Thus really Newman, perhaps almost unconsciously does not place enough reliance on the authority of the Church and if he were sailing in the direction of the rocks of Modernism, he might have found it difficult to pay sufficient homage to the Church built on the Rock.

Dean Inge shall give us in a quotation, the character of Newman and I will then endeavour to sum up the subject of this Essay.

" The character of Newman may seem to have been more admirable than lovable. He was more apt to make disciples than friends. Yet he was loved and honoured by men whose love is an honour and he is admired by all who can appreciate a consistently unworldly life. The Roman Church has been less unpopular in England since Newman received from it the highest honour it can bestow. That his life is for the most part a record of sadness and failure is no indication that he was not one of the great men of his time. He has stirred movements which still agitate the Church of England and the Church of Rome, and the end of which is not yet in sight. Anglo-Catholicism and Modernism are alien growths, perhaps, in the institutions where they have found a place ; but the man who beyond all others is responsible for grafting them upon the old stems is secure of his place in history."

． ． ． ． ． ． ．

At the beginning of this Essay, I wrote that I thought Dean Inge had written one of the best considerations concerning Cardinal Newman that existed. I think that is so, because of the fact that, in my opinion, it is a consideration that is above all, out for the whole truth. The Dean does not whitewash Newman, nor does he condemn him. He takes him as he is and we are introduced to a very complex personality who lived in very perplexing times. I have no intention of saying that Roman Catholic theologians make a habit of turning facts in their direction, but I do suggest that those who say Newman was supremely happy in that Church, have to find a wide application for the word happiness. As I have said, perhaps Newman was in a sense happy in the Roman Church. But this is not the same thing as saying that he would have been intensely unhappy in any other Church.

Dean Inge certainly shows that the Roman Church never trusted Newman or rather it never allowed him to put into active operation any educational schemes. It has always been rather a problem why the dignity of being created a Cardinal came to Newman. In a way it would make Newman, to succeeding generations, a more notable convert, than if he had been a mere Father Newman. I do not say this is so. But with great wisdom the Roman Church looks ahead and perchance it saw, when men around did not see, that Cardinal Newman would be one of those men about whom plain men would say " but there must be something in the Roman Church, see how it attracted Cardinal Newman." I say this may be an explanation of the curious dualism that makes a man who is only half a Catholic the proud possessor of the most conspicuous honour that body can give.

I would suggest, and I think that it is not contradictory to what Dean Inge says, that Newman could hardly have been happy in *any* Church. In any Church he would have been half for it, half against it. I do not mean that there is any indication in Newman that he was the type of man to create a " fancy " religion, but I mean, he was perhaps too great, too individualistic to be really at peace in any body which demanded adherence to a certain code of rules.

On the whole Dean Inge gives an impression that Newman was slightly disagreeable, not because he hated men but because he was probably immeasurably superior to them. That he was a very lonely person is obvious, whatever we think about Newman. But great men are usually lonely for the simple fact that they watch the crowd but are not of it. They see the mass of the people hurtle by but they stand afar off not through snobbishness but through sheer inability to " come down."

I think that there is no doubt that Inge is right in assuming that the interest in Newman felt by present day people, is to be explained by his queer personality and his almost contradictory mind. But this is not I think perhaps the whole reason. It is rather I think, in a great figure who wrote a great hymn, a hymn which expresses the longings of millions of people.

It may be that those who love Newman's hymn

and love him because of it, have no care whether he was a Protestant or whether he was a Catholic. It may be that those who love Newman have no interest in his great battle with Kingsley or his unpleasant relations with Manning. They may have no care that his Irish University failed, they may not even be interested as to why Newman became a Cardinal.

They may not even be interested in what Dean Inge thinks about Newman or his contention that the interest in him, is explained by himself.

No, it may be that they love Newman because of my old man who sings in my Square on Summer Evenings. If Newman had only written "Lead, Kindly Light," the ordinary people might still have been attracted by him. Perhaps Dean Inge misses this point, but then the Dean can hardly be expected to see so ordinary a thing!

Whatever may be the real reason of the continued interest in Newman, Dean Inge has written a brilliant Essay on the man. And those who read his Essay with care need not view with any serious attention, the squeals of certain Catholic apologists who accuse Dean Inge of a want of good manners when dealing with men and things that belong to the Roman Church.

Instead, they may feel amazed that so poor a body as the Protestants can produce such fine understanding of another Church as is displayed by Dean Inge, when he discusses the great Cardinal Newman.

END OF PEEP TWO.

Peep Number Three.

MAX BEERBOHM, SWINBURNE, AND OTHER THINGS.

MR. BEERBOHM in writing about Swinburne makes the remark that " in my youth the suburbs were rather looked down on—I never quite knew why." In this respect Mr. Beerbohm seems a little simple. The suburbs are looked down upon because they contain all the flotsam and jetsam that isn't quite society. I suppose the inhabitants of suburbs might well be divided into two classes, those who are snobs and those who are not, and there is no doubt whatever that the former class preponderate !

Mr. Beerbohm goes on to say that it was a matter for making merry that Swinburne lived in a suburb. As if it mattered in the very slightest, if that terrific genius lived in Putney or Poplar, what mattered and does matter is that a very wise and all seeing God chose to create a Swinburne that small men might pause and wonder how immense can be the glory of one poet. Mr. Beerbohm is much more right when he expresses surprise that Swinburne lived at all. What he means, I suppose, is that it is remarkable that he lived so long, seeing that he lived so frankly and in the way that he chose, whether men agreed to his choosing or whether they did not.

To enter into a digression before I say something of Beerbohm's meeting with Swinburne at the Pines. It concerns Keats, that sorrowful person who seemed born on a Cross, a Cross of misunderstanding and harshness. This is what Beerbohm says of him and it is an unkind and unjust thing to say and in any case a veiled sneer at Keats is not quite done.

This is what Beerbohm writes :

" A great part of Keats' fame rests on our assumption of what he *would* have done."

This is purely smart gossip which has no ring of truth in it. Keats has his fame for what he did, for wise critics are they who do not deny fame to a poet because he dies before his years are very many. Now if Beerbohm had made this remark about some of the war poets, especially Rupert Brooke, there is some truth in it. Brooke lived because he died, the war which killed him made him live. I of course think that had he lived he would have produced much notable work. But the suggestion of " might have done " about Keats is beside the point and Beerbohm ought to know better.

But away to The Pines, away with Beerbohm at his best. A visit to Swinburne. And, ye Gods, in the most prosaic of suburbs. Putney, just where London begins.

Here is a delicious picture of Beerbohm getting near to the residence at which Swinburne lived.

" Out here were all the aspects of common modern life. In there was Swinburne. A butcher-boy went by, whistling. He was not going to see Swinburne."

Of course he was not. He had more important work to do, beef for the worthy rector, mutton for the zealous doctor, twenty steaks for twenty plebeian housewives, thirty chops for thirty souls, who would probably care as much for Swinburne as a shop girl cares for the philosophy of Bergson. Oh, dreadful modern life that it should be a truism that the butcher's boy is more important than an astounding poet, that the blood of violent poetry should be of less account than the blood of recently violently killed beef. And yet, if we are really determined to be true to truth, the world of suburb could live without Swinburne but not without the butcher's boy. But my contention is true, how dreadful is modern life, that we must prefer meat to poetry, the food of the body to the food of the soul.

But we will leave the butcher's boy to whistle, and whistling is the most glorious sound in all the world, and be with Beerbohm at the great moment when he meets the poet.

And what a moment it is when we meet the man we have perchance thought about all our life, what desperate rapture it may be, what appalling disappointment may be the result of the meeting, the meeting may be something that we remember until we slip away out of things remembered, the meeting may be something that for ever makes us sad, for we met the great man but once ere he was so swiftly borne away.

But, Beerbohm was not disappointed. The journey to Putney had not been in vain, the spectacle of the whistling butcher's boy had done no harm. A great event in the life of Max Beerbohm, a sudden seeing of that thunderous poet, a sudden contact with a man of amazing genius.

"Nor was I disappointed. Swinburne's entry was for me a great moment. Here, suddenly visible in the flesh was the legendary being and divine singer. Here he was, shutting the door behind him as might anybody else, and advancing a strange small figure in grey having an air at once noble and roguish, proud and skittish. My name was roared to him. In shaking his hand I bowed low of course—a *bow de coeur* ; and he, in the old aristocratic manner, bowed equally low, but with such swiftness that we narrowly escaped concussion."

There has always been much interest about the look of Swinburne, we like to know the hands, feet, and heads of great men. We expect them to be somewhat different and are disappointed if it so happens that their limbs are as the limbs of humbler beings. And it is quite certain, that quite often physical eccentricity does accompany unusual mental powers. It certainly did in the case of Swinburne. It was not that he *was* something out of the ordinary, he certainly *looked* it.

Mr. Beerbohm gives a detailed description of the poet and it is certainly no worse than many others.

In figure, at first glance, he seemed almost fat but this was merely because of the way he carried himself, with his long neck strained so tightly back that he all receded from the waist upwards. I noticed afterwards that this deportment made the back of his jacket hang quite far away from his legs ; and so small and sloping were his shoulders that the jacket seemed ever so likely to slip right off. His hands were tiny even for his size and they fluttered, helplessly, touchingly unceasingly."

This description brings out with some force the artistic powers of Mr. Beerbohm. The detail is full but it is not unnecessary. There is enough to paint a picture but not a lot of " extras " thrown in.

Those who are familiar with the appearance of Swinburne will probably agree that Mr. Beerbohm has painted an accurate picture.

Mr. Beerbohm is the type of Essayist who writes so smoothly that it is a little difficult to realise that he is saying a great deal, so little is the apparent effort. Here is a perfectly natural description of the poet at his meal. We get in a few sentences the relationship between Swinburne and Watts Dunton. It is one of those easy familiar scenes when two men are very close together.

" So soon as the mutton had been replaced by the apple pie, Watts-Dunton leaned and " Well, Algernon," he roared, " how was it on the heath

to-day ? " Swinburne, who had meekly inclined
his ear to the question, now threw back his head,
uttering a sound that was like the cooing of a dove
and forthwith, rapidly, ever so musically, he spoke
to us of his walk ; spoke not in the strain of a man
who had been taking his daily exercise on Putney
Heath but rather in that of a Peri who had at long
last been suffered to pass through Paradise."

A little later on, when Swinburne had gone to
write, for nothing must break his methodical day,
we get another good insight of Watts-Dunton and
Swinburne.

It is a glorious friendship for what better than
to have literally dragged a man of genius from
slaying himself ? And to have saved Swinburne
is to intensify the greatness of the rescue, a
thousandfold. It is no wonder that Watts-
Dunton is known and ever will be known as
" the friend of Swinburne," it might be that it
would be more accurate to call him the saviour of
Swinburne. This is what Beerbohm feels about
the friendship between these two men.

" Some twenty years had passed since that night,
when ailing and broken—thought to be nearly
dying, Watts-Dunton told me, Swinburne was
brought in a four-wheeler to The Pines. Regular
private nursing homes either did not exist in those
days or were less in vogue than they are now.
The Pines was to be a sort of private nursing home
for Swinburne. It was a good one. He recovered. He was most grateful to his friend and
saviour. He made as though to depart, was

persuaded to stay a little longer, and then a little longer than that. But I rather fancy that to the last, he never did, in the fullness of his modesty and good manners, consent to regard his presence as a matter of course or as anything but a terminable intrusion and obligation. His bow seemed always to convey that."

Thus very delicately, very gently, almost tenderly, does Beerbohm tell of the obligation of Swinburne to Watts-Dunton. It was an obligation that could not be paid in words, it was far too sacred for that, it could only be acknowledged by a splendid gesture. The courtly bow, a wealth of meaning in the sincere symbol, that no words could express with the same emphasis. It is delightful and it is something more, in this world of chaos to ruminate on the wonderful friendship that lasted so long at number two The Pines. It is these kind of friendships, little said may be on either side, little said because words express so little, it is I say, these friendships that spread their radiance throughout the darkness of the world. It is these literary friendships which make men pause and wonder and ask incredulously, what is this brotherhood that makes men cling together so that nothing shall separate them until one has to obey the summons and follow the road that disappears out of mortal sight.

One more glimpse of the meeting between Beerbohm and Swinburne and I must away to other matters, and they must have their turn. I will end with a wish that perhaps is uppermost in the

minds of all literary men, a wish that there may be
a meeting the other side of the impenetrable
river. The wish is expressed rather curiously by
Mr. Beerbohm.

But it is a little wistful for Mr. Beerbohm
isn't quite sure that he will meet Swinburne on the
other side and who is sure ? Certainly not those
who think the most ?

" I wish I had Watt-Dunton's sure faith in
meetings beyond the grave. I am glad I do not
disbelieve that people may so meet. I like to
think that some day in Elysium I shall—not
without diffidence—approach those two and re-
introduce myself."

And at least it is more helpful and I think on
most grounds more reasonable, to think that there
will be this meeting on the other side of the grave.
For it could surely not be that death destroyed a
friendship, the very essence of which is love at its
very highest. But I leave this to the theologians
full knowing that they cannot convince because they
must believe such a meeting can take place or leave
off being theologians. But perhaps all speculation
is useless, perhaps the Catholic Church in her
teachings of the unseen world is to be trusted. But
I cannot think that Swinburne would like to be
proved alive somewhere by the findings of theology !

. . . .

Let us consider Beerbohm discussing the question
of going for a walk. What a subject, to be happy
about, what a subject about which to weep. Do

you remember walking when you were quite young, do you remember how the sun shone, how the roads seemed white, how you skipped along ?

Then years after, you walked but you walked no longer alone. You walked with someone and the sun shone more brightly, the road seemed more white and your footsteps danced to the music of a great joy. Then years after, you again walked alone, and in the distance the great clouds rolled up, the road seemed black, your footsteps could hardly shuffle along.

However Berbohm quite obviously does not like walking, to get out of it, he has to make a very feeble excuse, it lands him in certain dilemmas, but it allows us to partake of his delicious humour.

" It is easy to say simply ' No ' to an old friend. In the case of a mere acquaintance one wants some excuse. ' I wish I could,' but—nothing ever occurs to me except ' I have some letters to write ! '' This formula is unsatisfactory in three ways. (1) It isn't believed. (2) It compels you to rise from your chair, go to the writing table and sit improvising a letter to somebody until the walkmonger (just not daring to call you liar and hypocrite) shall have lumbered out of the room. (3) It won't operate on Sunday mornings. ' There's no post out till this evening ' clinches the matter ; and you may as well go quietly.''

In fact according to Max Beerbohm the very process of walking deadens the brain and the conversation resulted in, becomes tedious. This is what apparently happens to a clever man when he takes a walk.

" He says that A (our host) is a thoroughly good fellow. Fifty yards further on, he adds that, A is one of the best fellows he has ever met. We tramp another furlong or so and he says that Mrs. A is a charming woman. Presently he adds that she is one of the most charming women he has ever known."

But Mr. Beerbohm is a little pessimistic. The last time I went for a walk, a glorious walk down Marlow way, my companion and I discussed the Immaculate Conception and then, but a mile or so on, the dazzling whiteness of a maiden's legs ; across the Thames she displayed them in all their comeliness, and the topic of their perfection lasted until our house was gained and lunch, a welcome interruption !

And the reason that Mr. Beerbohm is of the opinion that going out for a walk deadens the brain is that the brain doesn't quite approve of the body taking this violent and arbitrary exercise. On a walk then there is a kind of quarrel between the brain and the body.

" The body is going out because the mere fact of its doing so is a sure indication of nobility, probity and rugged grandeur of character—very well Vagula, have your own wayula ! But I say the brain flatly refuses to be mixed up in this tomfoolery. I shall go to sleep till it is over. The brain then wraps itself up in its own convolutions, and falls into a dreamless slumber from which nothing can arouse it till the body has been safely deposited indoors again."

Thus, you must take warning of the terrible effects of walking and your money must be expended in riding in a carriage or a motor and the brain will not then protest and relapse into a gloomy and morose lethargy.

. . . .

In an admirable Essay on Servants, Mr. Beerbohm discusses in passing the reason that servants are better treated to-day. The question that arises is whether servants *are* treated better. Probably they are, but no merit whatever divulges on employers. It is quite simply that very fortunately servants will not be badly treated. They have a place in the universe and they have no intention of the extent of that universe being some filthy diabolical basement kitchen with an environment of a vile beast of a mistress and a perspective of six stone steps. No, they insist on being treated as human beings. Not that all mistress were bad, they were not, the old family servant has been one of the many glories of England But far too many mistresses and masters for that, treated the servants as if they were an inferior class of beings, specially created to work for the lowest wages and be the recipient of cold orders and tough cold mutton.

Mr. Beerbohm traces the better conditions prevailing for servants, to the fact that they themselves have secured an amelioration of their lot. Mr. Beerbohm explains he is not a sociologist, but as an Essayist he says a good many very sociological things. This, about the better conditions for those who serve, is one of them.

Mr. Beerbohm asks why it is that domestic service is not so unpopular as it was.

" In other words, how is that servants have so much less unpleasant a time they they were having half a century ago ? I should like to think this melioration came through our sense of justice, but I cannot claim that it did. Somehow, our sense of justice never turns in its sleep till long after the sense of injustice in others has been thoroughly aroused ; nor is it ever up and doing till those others have begun to make themselves thoroughly disagreeable and not even then will it be up and doing more than is urgently required of it by our inconvenience at the moment."

Then Mr. Beerbohm comes down from the general to the particular.

" For the improvement in their lot, servants must, I am afraid, be allowed to thank themselves rather than their employers."

This is an unpleasant judgment, that we only wish to help others to save ourselves inconvenience. But I am afraid that this is characteristic of the Englishman. We see it is the case of all the glorious hypocrisy that has been talked about Belgium. If we had had any idea that Germany had no desire to attack us after she had passed through Belgium and swamped France, we should have been reluctant to stir a finger. But the

English nation knew that to make itself quite safe, Belgium must be helped but it had nothing whatever to do with honour. Honour to an Englishman is something that has to be indulged in to save trouble. So, when our servants began to get assertive we said that they, poor things, must be better looked after. We will not force them to go to Church, and there, sit in the worst seats in the building, they shall not be forced to come in at ten o'clock, they shall be allowed to know that there is a world beyond the kitchen steps, not because we cared one jot about our servants, the English are much too superior to care for mere domestics, but it would be so unplesant to have no servants, so they, poor ill treated creatures, must be treated as well as is necessary to ensure that they work for us. Yes, Mr. Beerbohm knows our national indifference to bad conditions for other people and it is perhaps this failing which has made foreigners say that the English are a nation of hypocrites. We are, but our greatness has been founded on it. For the English if they are hypocritical are also clever. In a word the Englishman (as a national character, not the individual Englishman) is a clever hypocrite. It is not his fault, it is his birthright and probably comes from a feeling of innate piety.

The Englishman is pious in so far as he feels that it is incumbent on himself to play the role of the very highly civilised being. I wish it were otherwise but I am quite convinced that Mr. Beerbohm is right in his suggestion that we only wish for better conditions for other people, so that " other people " shall not grow tired of our inhumanity and turn round and utterly slay us.

.   .   .   .

I think in some ways, Mr. Beerbohm is one of the most delightful of our essayists. With a profundity of wisdom for the most part, he chatters delightfully. You can almost see the joy in which the neatly proportioned phrases drop from his fertile pen. All sorts of subjects he deals with for his Essays. The Essay to him is a pleasant means of literary expression, there is a geniality about his writing, though he can hit hard and hit so hard that the blow suddenly staggers.

If it be pleaded that a great deal of Mr. Beerbohm's work is journalism then it merely postulates what a fine thing journalism really is and at its best a very close relation to that elusive and undefined divine entity which men call literature. Perhaps Mr. Beerbohm is a very literary journalist, that is, he combines the *flair* for catching hold of the everyday things and turning them into delicate yet straightforward prose.

I am not sure whether I like Mr. Beerbohm better when he is angry than when his writing radiates a pleasant smile. When he is angry, he is angry in a good cause (to whit our hypocrisy about the servant treatment question) when he smiles, he smiles because life amuses him and perhaps his laughter gets a little near to tears at times. Good indeed, is it, when the Essayist can make us laugh and yet feel in our pockets to see whether that handkerchief is somewhere in the vicinity. Good indeed, is it, when a literary person such as Beerbohm can demand that his gloom, when left alone in a dull cottage, can only be appeased by books. For books keep us from suicide yet they may drive us to take our life in sheer despair at the things men can never know.

But for Beerbohm books are a solace, a " very pleasant help in trouble " for Beerbohm says that he hates to be alone. Yet one can never really be alone, why it is when one has only one's soul to talk to, that all the great thoughts are talked. What has produced the books that make our world such a charming place ? A great and maddening solitude, for when men fear very greatly, when they suddenly think that one day they will pass out of the world, then comes the mood for writing, for you cannot be alone in the more terrible sense if you write.

And what is the purpose of the Essays that Mr. Beerbohm writes ? It would not perhaps be too hazardous, too impertinent, too savouring of in- quisitiveness to suggest a reason. May be ; it is that Mr. Beerbohm knows life to be crowded with events and situations that demand to be shown to other people. The Essayist, the literary journalist, such as Mr. Beerbohm, is unsefish. Vast impressions and simple thoughts come into his mind, why should they not come into and help the minds of other people ? They shall do this thing. Such I dare to suggest is the mental process of Mr. Beerbohm. These thoughts shall be put into permanent form.

Think what we should have missed if Mr. Beerbohm had kept to himself the visit to Swinburne. Think what we should have missed if Dickens had never allowed us to weep hot tears of anguish at poor Scrooge, think what we should have missed if Thackeray had not allowed us to be the witnesses of the death of Colonel Newcome.

So like all Essayists of the oddities of life, Mr. Beerbohm is unsefish. His charming Essays are the reflection of a subtle and observing mind. In Mr. Beerbohm are delightfully blended all that is best in the rather vague term which struts about the world and is known as Literary Journalism.

END OF PEEP THREE.

Peep Number Four.

A. C. BENSON and THE THREAD OF GOLD.

SINCE the very lamented death of the Master of Magdalene College, Cambridge, certain critics while admitting the charm of Mr. Benson's writings, have added at the same time, that they savour of superficiality. Now, I have an idea that these critics have rather confused simplicity with superficiality. Rather, I go further and say that Mr. Benson is profound. He is profound because he is simple, his truths, his problems are not dressed up in ornate trappings, nor are they unclothed and mere skeletons ; they are put down in a straightforward way. Taking rather at random, one of his most popular books of Essays, " The Thread of Gold," I shall endeavour in this Essay to examine Mr. Benson's methods and approach to certain incidents and lines of thought. I have been influenced in my choice by the question of diverseness, for Mr. Benson had a wide mind, if I may use the term in the sense that he wrote about a wide area of human tribulation, human joy and human activity. And I suggest that his mind was not only wide, it was also deep.

Let me start for examination with something about melancholy. For all through the book this divine stream wends its way. I say divine, for melancholy is the fairest of the gifts of the gods. She can be seen in the gentle rain which sweeps down over the hills spreading a mist that appears like a soft garment, she can be seen when the sun shines on the blue sea and in the distance makes gold, the big ships that are going to the other ends of the earth, she can be seen hiding just away in the distance, when all is joy, waiting to calm the reaction that might otherwise lead to a violent despair. For melancholy is not violent, she is serene, she is not angry, she is merely rather sad, she hovers over all nature and poets define her nature.

I never read Mr. Benson without feeling that here we have a melancholy man, a melancholy man because a man of great unselfishness, because a man of vast imagination, because, a man of depth of soul. If the critics who call Mr. Benson superficial would study his melancholy, they would find that the charge of superficiality had in it a distinct recoil. For the melancholy of Mr. Benson is the best type. He calls it Leucocholy. It is the gentle melancholy for which I hold so strong a brief.

This is how Mr. Benson writes of the divine mood. It comes in the nature of a friend.

" I have had to taste, during the last few days, I know not why, the cup of what Gray called Leucocholy ; it is not Melancholy, only the pale shadow of it. It sends flowing through the mind a gentle current of sad and weary images and thoughts, which still have a beauty of their own ; it tinges one's life with a sober greyness of hue ; it heightens perception, though it prevents enjoyment."

This last statement in my opinion is utterly untrue, I believe it is quite possible to thoroughly enjoy melancholy, if it is not, how is it that so much poetry is read ? How is it that Barrie can get thousands to listen to his plays ? How is it that the Church has made the central part of Christianity the bone in the whole essence of the story ? How is that we love the sad sea waves, if their sadness or melancholy did not produce pleasurable emotions ? And I refuse to concede that to enjoy melancholy is a form of morbid excitement, I contend that it is an appreciation of the essential bedrock of things. Of course it may be said that at times melancholy leads to that pernicious emotion of despair, but it often leads not to despair but to joy. Joy is the reaction of melancholy, melancholy is the reaction of joy. And I believe melancholy is a finer emotion. Mr. Benson himself says after his fit of melancholy has lifted :

" To-day, little by little, the cloudy mood drew off and left me smiling. The love of the peaceful and patient earth came to comfort me. How pure and free were the long lines of ploughland, the broad back of the gently-swelling down ! " And Mr. Benson cannot quite think where his sad mood

has gone, perchance it has gone to kiss someone
else far away.

" Where was my sad mood gone ? The clear
air seemed to have blown through my mind,
hands had been waved to me from leafless woods,
quiet voices of field and stream had whispered
me their secrets ; " We would tell, if we could,"
they seemed to say. And I listening, had learnt
patience, too—for awhile."

That is perhaps the supreme lesson of melancholy, patience ; that things change, joy is not
for ever, melancholy is not for ever, we must
sometimes be sad and we must sometimes enjoy
this sadness. For there is indeed laughter in
tears and, so much more, tears in laughter.

.   .   .   .

I have always been most interested in an adventure Mr. Benson appears to have had with a
beetle. The adventure opens up a most terrific
problem. The beetle met Mr. Benson's eye, the
eye killed the beetle, therein lies the problem.
Mr. Benson deals with it in this manner.

" It was such a trifling thing after all. I was
bicycling very pleasantly down a country road
to-day, when one of those small pungent beetles,
a tiny thing in black plate-armour, for all the
world like a minute torpedo, sailed straight into
my eye. The eyelid, quicker even than my own
thought shut itself down but too late. The little
fellow was engulphed in what Walt Whitman
would call the liquid rim."

Here then is the simple problem that might occur a thousand times, on a thousand country roads any fine day you like to mention. This is how the incident set Mr. Benson thinking. It leads to a perfectly insoluble problem.

" Now, that is not a very marvellous incident ; but it set me wondering. In the first place, what a horrible experience for the creature ; in a moment as he sailed joyfully along, saying " Aha " perhaps, like the war horse among the trumpets, on the scented summer breeze with the sun warm on his mail, to find himself stuck fast in a hot and oozy crevice, and presently to be crushed to death. His little taste of the pleasant world so soon over, and for me an agreeable hour spoilt, so far as I could see, to no particular purpose." So the small incident leads to speculation about the love of God. It worries Mr. Benson as it has worried and will worry millions of other people, who can see no purpose in the apparently senseless acts of cruelty that take place every minute. This is not melancholy, make no mistake about it, this thought soons leads to despair or, which is much more frequent, " oh well, there you are, there is no solution, lets leave it alone, let us eat drink and be merry, for to-morrow—plenty of time to worry to-morrow."

But not so Mr. Benson, the beetle sets in motion a depressing line of thought. I have a very good idea that it pursued the brilliant kindly Essayist until his death.

" If God is omnipotent and all-loving, we are

bound to believe that suffering and death are sent
by him deliberately and not cruelly. One single
instance, however minute, that established the
reverse, would vitiate the whole theory; and if
so, then we are the sport of a power that is sometimes kind and sometimes malignant. An in-
supportable thought."

But, are we not born in the image of God, are
we not sometimes kind, sometimes malignant?
We cannot start a parallelism and not finish it.
We cannot say that God is only like us in so far
as He is kind, it may be that He is like us, in so
far as we are cruel. Unpleasant I admit, but
there you are.

And here comes in the desperate sorrow of the
whole thing. Mr. Benson can offer no solution.
Who can?

" What, then, is my solution? That is the
melancholy part of it; I am not prepared to offer
one."

And yet perhaps, were there to be a solution, it
would be more melancholy. Mr. Benson has said
that melancholy leads to patience. Perhaps yet
again, patience is the answer. It is in so many
things in life. We are with Mr. Benson in a black
mood here, one of those dreadful moments when
all is thick fog, so thick that we shall choke,
so thick that we cannot remember where we have
come from and where we have to go.

" I am met on every side by hopeless difficulties.
I am tempted to think that God is not at all what
we imagine him to be; that our conceptions of

benevolence and justice and love are not necessarily
true of him at all."

Yes, but there is the converse and here Mr.
Benson does seem a little superficial. If our
conception concerning the benevolence of God be
wrong (as Mr. Benson suggests) why not that our
conception of his possible cruelty be wrong also ?

For after all we have not yet determined at all
what cruelty really is, it is a most indubitably
evolutionary concept.

And yet the position is not quite hopeless, for
Mr. Benson writes :

"And thus I rest in the trust that there is somewhere, far off a beauty and a joy in suffering; and that,
perhaps, death itself is a fair and desirable thing."

Not perhaps a very original conclusion but
probably the only possible one. Then Mr. Benson
is extremely dogmatic, for he says that the " poor
beetle knows about it now." Perhaps Mr. Benson
and the beetle have met again, and perhaps the
beetle has told him that he bears him no grudge
for his premature death, perhaps even, it may be
that the beetle has said that his death was neither
premature nor the spite of a cruel and illogical God.

So like most problems, there is a possible way
out, or in other words a refuge from a deep and
bitter depair. Perhaps again that the Infinite
Mind of the Universe is not cruel but inscrutable for
inscrutability looks so much like cruelty that they
become mixed up. In fact, we must not grieve
too much for the beetle who died so suddenly
and so violently in the eye of Mr. Benson.

It is always a matter of the supremest interest
to know what a man thinks about his own trade
or profession. We like to hear what a jockey
thinks about the profession of jockeyship, we are
glad to know how an executioner regards his own
work. He may think quite differently about it
to those who are outside. The public may
imagine that an executioner is a bit of a brute
whereas I believe that he himself considers his
profession to be honourable and utilitarian ! Now
it is especially interesting to know what an author
thinks about his own work. Many people who
are not authors (and even in these days one or
two people do not write) regard the profession as a
gigantic hobby. That it is serious and hard work
comes to them as a bit of surprise. That is
perhaps quite natural, the finished book looks so
easily done. People think it is nice and comfortable to merely write books and become written
of in all the newspapers. Authorship appears
to many as a sort of perpetual amusement, " It
must be so charming," they say, " to write novels."
So it is ; and the most charming part is when
they are written and past that fiend in human
form the publisher's reader. All this gossip about
what people think of their own work has been
occasioned by the fact that Mr. Benson writes
of his own work, in that he writes of authorship.

Mr. Benson has no belief in worrying too much
over writing, in the sense of being over anxious
or unduly pedantic.

" To be honest, I do not believe in fretting too

much over a piece of writing. Writing, laboriously constructed, painfully ornamented, is often I think both laborious and painful to read ; there is a sense of strain about it."

I think that quite generally speaking this is true enough. Much of the best work that is done by the pen, is that which comes straight, almost with a rush, from the brain, via the pen, down to the paper.

Then there is the question of how long at a stretch a writer should work. This is of course largely depends upon the writer. Many people do not realise how great is the physical strain of writing, the strain of sitting in one chair hour after hour, the strain of thinking and producing thought at almost the same moment. Again it entirely depends upon what is being written. Mr. Benson does not advise very long hours of work. But it has to be remembered that Mr. Benson could not have been called a strong man. His advice on the matter of the length of time that one should write at a stretch is well worth quoting.

" I do not think that one can write for very long to much purpose ; I take the two or three hours when the mind is clearest and freshest, and write as rapidly as I can ; this secures, it seems to me, a clearness and a unity which cannot be attained by fretful labour, by poking and pinching at one's work. One avoids by rapidity and ardour the dangerous defect of repetition ; a big task must be divided into small sharp episodes to be thus swiftly treated."

This seems to me to be extraordinarily important. The arrangement of a piece of writing, is, in my opinion, of much more consequence than the actual style. It is easier to follow a confused style than a confused arrangement. It is better for the reader if the work before him is well arranged than if it is merely well written with no plan whatever. Naturally the ideal is a good style and a good arrangement. But where one only can be obtained, I believe that arrangement is the most important.

Of the joy of writing Mr. Benson experiences in no small measure. It is to him a very delightful occupation.

" I am speaking here very frankly ; and I will own that for myself, when the day has rolled past and when the sacred hour comes, I sit down to write with an appetite, a keen rapture such as a hungry man may feel when he sits down to a savoury meal."

And it may be said here that the writing of Mr. Benson gives the impression of being the work of someone who is in love with his work. We can inagine the busy Cambridge scholar, away up in the glorious quiet of a University town, passing away the hours in these Essays about all the miscellaneous things that came into his mind. So rapidly does hc pass from one subject to another, that we feel his mind was absorbed by a perpetual and enthusiastic energy. And this energy could quite obviously only be expelled by eager and unrestrained writing. Of course the case of the professional writer is not quite the same. He cannot wait for a mood, any more than the bank clerk can wait for a mood to start him to his daily work. The professional writer (and I do not mean by this the journalist), must write day in, day out, if he is to attain to anything at all. He cannot wait until he is hungry enough to wish to satisfy the writing hunger, he must write quite often just mechanically, because (to use a mealtime symbolism), it is writing time. And very often he produces quite as good work as the man who only writes when the overpowering mood is upon him.

Then Mr. Benson says something which sounds very magnanimous and very unselfish and very fine, but like many fine sounding things, there is no bedrock of truth in the saying. He writes :

" But the essence of the happ'ness is that the joy resides in the doing of the work and not in the giving it to the world."

This is pure eyewash and pure rubbish. The joy of literary work is in the publishing of it, the making of the rough sheets of manuscript into a book which will adorn many bookcases. If the joy of writing merely lay in the writing, how is it that hundreds of people go down to a miserable despair because their manuscripts live and die in the bottom drawer in the back room ? How is it that publishers and editors are inundated with unsuitable work, if people find the joy of writing sufficient in itself ? No, Mr. Benson is utterly wrong and if he were right three-quarters

of the books that are published would remain as
manuscripts to the infinite loss of many people.
For I am no believer that much bad work is really
published, I believe, much more, that bad work
is unpublished !

From a discussion of authorship, it is appropri-
ate enough to go on to examine something of what
Mr. Benson says of Wordsworth. Mr. Benson
has a great deal to say about this poet which is
both interesting and true. But I cannot say
that Mr. Benson makes Wordsworth out to be a
particularly attractive personality in some ways.
And this was not because the poet was vicious or
even disagreeable but rather that he was full of an
unbounded self-satisfaction. So many poets have
seemed to be the most dissatisfied of men, that we
are a little annoyed to discover one who was not.
This is how Mr. Benson writes of the self-sufficiency
of Wordsworth.

" Wordsworth, indeed, was armed at all points
by a strong and simple pride, too strong to be
vanity, too simple to be egotism. He is one of
the few supremely fortunate men in the history of
literature, because he had none of the sensitiveness
or indecision that are so often the curse of the
artistic temperament."

How true in every sense is this, not only concerning Wordsworth but concerning the general
principle of the sensitiveness of artistic people.
The world little knows how those who are really
artistic shudder at its gross vulgarity, its absurd
conventions, its contempt of all that is beautiful, its

hideous commercialism and snobbery, its utter
disregard for anything except itself.

With regard to Wordsworth, the reason of his
self-sufficiency was, according to Mr. Benson, that
he was never particularly interested in anyone.
An excellent maxim if you would shun sorrow, for
if you never love deeply, you can never miss
deeply. And perhaps it is better to love slenderly
and miss slenderly than to love overwhelmingly
and then be overwhelmed and crushed utterly
when the inevitable time for parting comes.
Here is a really brilliant picture of the " evenness "
of Wordsworth.

" He bore himself with the same homely dignity
in all companies alike ; he was never particularly
interested in anyone, he never had any fear of
being thought ridiculous or pompous. His favourite reading was his own poetry, he wished
everyone to be interested in his work, because
he was conscious of its supreme importance. He
probably made the mistake of thinking that it
was his sense of poetry and beauty that made him
simple and tranquil."

But he was not this at all, thinks Mr. Benson.
In all probability whatever Wordsworth had done
he would have been contented for :

" It was the simplicity and tranquility of his
temperament that gave him the power of enjoyment in so large a measure."

And again how kind a critic is Mr. Benson. How
well does he always blend praise with his slight
condemnation. If he has to concede that Words-

worth was self-satisfied and slightly pompous,
we must be told at the same time of the nobility of
his life, his gentleness and his pilgrimage of wonder
in the hills and lakes that were his background.

" And yet what a fine, pure, noble, gentle life
it was ! The very thought of him, faring quietly
about among his hills and lakes, murmuring his
calm verse, in a sober and temperate joy, looking
everywhere for the same grave qualities among
quiet homekeeping folk, brings with it a high
inspiration. But we tend to think of Wordsworth
as a father and priest rather than as a brother and
a friend."

Which says only too truly that a priest is not a
brother but a leader, someone remote yet in a
sense a kind of father. Something like the idea
that we have of the Fatherhood of God and the
Priest " for ever after the order of Melchisedec."

Once more, for Mr. Benson, Wordsworth was a
really contented man, he accepted the mysteries
of the world and did not fret about them. How
different to the writer of the book that I am
attempting to examine. In Mr. Benson we see the
type of man who is always discontented, the
mysteries that he cannot hope to solve, perplex
and annoy him. They produce in him a state of
hopelessness, though it is true the sun shines
sooner or later. But his temperament is the very
opposite to that of Wordsworth. In the poet we see
transquillity and acceptance personified. In Mr.
Benson we see the sorrowing mind at the problems
of the universe, we see the moods of dark despair

and then the sudden glimmers of light, we see the sky obscured by dark masses of black cloud, then suddenly there is a break, the sun shines through, the birds break into song again and the outlook is not so hopeless. But these fits of hopelessness take heavy toll of a man, they took heavy toll of Mr. Benson, we can see through " The Thread of Gold " the fight that he has to retain his faith. It is a sombre spectacle but one of great courage.

In the few pages more that I can give to this Essay may I be permitted to say something about Mr. Benson's thoughts about religious matters and the question of Christ.

This is what Mr. Benson writes concerning the position of his belief in Christ.

" When I come to the New Testament I feel myself in the Gospels, confronted by the most wonderful personality which has ever drawn breath upon the earth."

There is nothing of much importance in this statement, it has been made again and again but It is interesting as expressing the Christological position of Mr. Benson.

Of all the fascinating parts of the Bible, and the Bible is really much more fascinating than the modern sex novel, perhaps the most fascinating is the last chapter of the Gospel which in my opinion is very rightly attributed to Saint John. After all it would be difficult to lean on the breast of Jesus and know nothing about Him. This chapter " bewilders " Mr. Benson. He writes of it in this most charming manner.

" It is bewildering, because it is a postscript, added, with a single artlessness, after the Gospel has come to a full close. Perhaps Saint John did not even write it, though the pretty childlike conclusion about the world itself not being able to contain the books that might be written about Christ has always seemed to me to be in his spirit, the words of a very simple minded and aged man."

It might well be added, that if it is true that the world could not contain all the books that could be written about Christ, it is equally true that all the books which *have* been written about Christ have never decided exactly what He was.

Very wisely, Mr. Benson will not discuss the charge to Saint Peter, that terrible question as to whether the Catholic claims are justified. Patience is perhaps again the only solution and a hope that we shall really know one day.

.   .   .   .

At the beginning of this Essay I insisted that it was unfair to attribute superficiality to the writings of Mr. Benson. At the end of this short Essay concerning some considerations in " The Thread of Gold" I am still of the same opinion.

It would be ridiculous to claim for Mr. Benson any great originality of thought. I think it is quite possible that it is largely because there is not this originality of thought in his work, which has been the cause of the charge of superficiality. We live in an age in which anything at all platitudinous is shrieked at with huge merriment, but it is quite forgotten that if we shriek with laughter at platitudes we must howl boisterously at the Sermon on the Mount. And after all, most platitudes are true and sensible or they would not have become platitudes.

There is a certain sombreness over the work of Mr. Benson. I do not believe that he was really at all a happy man, he was probably far too sympathetic to be able to be possessed of happiness. Nature seems to him tinged with inscrutability and cruelty. The Face of God is often veiled and the face of Man is saddened by this veiling. Yet Mr. Benson is never hopeless, there is nothing of the black despair of Ibsen in his writings, or the savage cynicism of Swift. Mr. Benson is essentially kind, his work rings with good nature and he treats his reader as though he really wanted to help him.

There is, I think, something permanent about the writings of Mr. Benson. The permanence of the writings seem to me to lie in the fact that so much of them deal with beauty. It was often expressed by the Master of Magdalene College, Cambridge, the wish that he might write a beautiful book. In " The Thread of Gold " I think he has succeeded in his ambition.

The beauty of " The Thread of Gold " lies in its love for nature and again I say, its sorrow at the cruelty of much of it. The sweet peace of rural England pervades the whole book. There is the visit to the crippled man, in any village we can find such a man, perhaps not very far from the shadow of the old parish church. There is the quiet consideration about the Christian story, all dealt with carefully, with no originality about it, it is true. Then there is another visit to a blind man and a dreadful picture in one sense it is, of the frightful tragedies that hide themselves away in the little houses throughout England.

Life for Mr. Benson as I have said does not seem to be happy, it is rather a weary pilgrimage, yet at the end there is hope, the night is succeeded by the morning, the moon gives place to the sun. Perhaps I cannot do better than end this Essay with the last few lines from " The Thread of Gold." They contain the germ of a wonderful kindliness.

" God grant us so to live, in courage and trust, that when He calls us, we may pass willingly and with a quiet confidence to the gate that opens into tracts unknown."

END OF PEEP FOUR.

CHESTERTON AND SOME HISTORY.

IN an Essay of this description, dealing with a serious and extensive subject, it is quite necessary to indulge in the art of selection. Mr. Chesterton of course calls his history of England " A Short History of England," and the strangest part of the whole thing is, that it is, as histories go, remarkably short ! But it is far too long to deal with in an Essay except in the selective manner. I have therefore adopted the policy of selection and have chosen three themes which Mr. Chesterton has written about. The three I have chosen, have been chosen with some care and they are :

Firstly that period of history which has to do with the Crusades.

Secondly I have thought that it would be interesting to say something of what Mr. Chesterton means by Merry England.

Thirdly I have dealt with something which many people think is the reverse of merry, the Age of the Puritans.

Let us then start with a consideration of the

Crusades, those glorious episodes of chivalry and fanaticism.

. . . .

Mr. Chesterton has no sympathy with the ordinary idea that the schoolboy gets about Richard Coeur de Lion, from the ordinary text book of history. He thinks that it is suggested, that Richard's escape was something like a " schoolboy running away to sea." This is to a certain extent true, at school one did have the idea that the Crusades were a sort of curious adventure rather like the adventures of Robinson Crusoe, except that the Crusaders wore considerably more clothes, than the people Robinson Crusoe met in his wanderings.

In fact for Mr. Chesterton, the start for the Crusades was not in the least degree in the nature of a sort of schoolboy adventure, it was a very serious thing, " more like a responsible English man, now going to the front."

Of course to-day the Englishman starts to the front more as if he was going for a week-end to the continent. A taxi to Victoria, a last look at the women of dirty old London, a glance through all the magazines that specialise in women's legs, a chat about the six days that are over and then a prosaic progress across the English Channel, with but one, or possibly two, backward glances at the white cliffs that mark out the old and wonderful town of Dover.

But the start to the Crusades was a start for the

war front and the war front was holy because " Christendom was nearly one nation and the Front was the Holy Land."

Mr. Chesteron has a very illuminating and unusual reason for the Crusades. He writes thus of how they appeared to Europeans :

" The reason, was, of course, that the Crusades were, for all thoughtful Europeans, things of the highest statesmanship and the purest public spirit." Which is to say that they were a kind of patriotic gesture. But it was much more. The Crusade spirit was a fight against a monstrous (but not necessarily infamous) faith which had arisen in the East. Almost as a challenge, grew up in the East that mighty religion of Mahomet, that mighty religion which has filled the Northern part of Africa with wonderful temples and mosques which gleam in the startling sunlight, as though they held a volume of liquid fire. The rising of Mohamedanism, seems to Mr. Chesterton, to be something like this :

"Some six hundred years after Christianity sprang up in the East and swept westwards, another great faith arose in almost the same eastern lands and followed it like its gigantic shadow. Like a shadow at once a copy and contrary."

The definition of the creed of the Moslems is singularly lucid. In a few words Mr. Chesterton has defined it brilliantly. For he writes : " We call it Islam, or the creed of the Moslems ; and perhaps its most explanatory description is that it was the final flaming up of the accumulated

Orientalisms, perhaps of the accumulated Hebra-
isma, gradually rejected as the Church grew
more European or as Christianity turned into
Christendom. Its highest motive was a hatred of
idols and in its view Incarnation was itself an
idolatry."

In a very remarkable passage, Mr. Chesterton
analyses what Rome must have felt as she beheld
the growth of the creed of Islam. She would
have seen something that was in the nature of a
trespasser. In a sense, if you like it, the creed of
Islam would have appeared to Rome as something
occupying a very holy place and refusing to admit
that it was holy. This is how Mr. Chesterton puts
it.

" Rome herself did not worship herself as in the
pagan age. Rome herself looked Eastward to the
mysterious cradle of her creed, to a land of which
the very earth was called holy."

And this is what she saw, something that must
have made her shake with anger and in her shaking
throw off the Spirit that was to be the Crusades.

" She saw standing in the place that was her
earthly heaven a devouring giant out of the
deserts, to whom all places were the same "

Thus we can again analyse the nature of the
quarrel, a quarrel not between two faiths so much,
as one faith shocked and astounded at the un-
imaginativeness of the other faith.

In this manner does Mr. Chesterton put the
matter quite concisely.

" It was nothing so simple as a quarrel between

two men who both wanted Jerusalem. It was the
much deadlier quarrel between one man who wanted
it and another man who could not see why it was
wanted."

I have already said that Mr. Chesterton has no
sympathy with the popular idea among schoolboys
that Richard started for the Crusades, as though
he were off on an adventure on the high seas.
Mr. Chesterton has no doubt whatever that Richard
did gain much glory for England by his fightings
in the East. It is an example of how England
has been helped by those who have not stayed at
home. England is no doubt much helped by those
who do not travel out of her confines, but her
greatness has been caused by those who were not
afraid to travel and find death and glory many
thousands of leagues beyond her boundaries.
The Pearl set in the Silver Sea has come because
all through the ages men have set out over that
sea and have left the Pearl far behind them, but
in so doing, the Pearl has become more and more
rare. So Richard by his enterprise, by his Crusad-
ing, by his contempt of danger, added fresh glory
to England and immortality for himself.

" King Richard," writes Mr. Chesterton, " as
the typical Crusader did make a momentous
difference to England by gaining glory in the
East, instead of devoting himself conscientiously
to domestic politics in the manner of King John."

Again King Richard was something more than
a king, he was an epic, a personification of the age
of chivalry, as to-day the profiteer is a personi-

fication of bad breeding and poisonous manners.
Mr. Chesterton loves Richard for he loves chivalry
and all that it means.

" Richard was not only a knight but a trouba-
dour ; and culture and courtesy were linked up
with the idea of English valour."

To get the best idea of what the Crusade really
was Mr. Chesterton says that we should imagine
every Crusade was in effect a Children's Crusade.

It was a time of the likeness of Children because it was a time of vision.   The Crusades were
a splendid adventure, but they were more, they
were a very splendid and pure religion.   For Mr.
Chesterton, then, they were not so much a fight
against Islam, as a fight against the very un-
imaginative pragmatism of Islam.   They were also
a very splendid expression of the chivalry and
valour of England.   And they were perhaps personified in Richard Coeur de Lion.

Again, and it must be the last thing that I can
here say of Mr. Chesterton and the Crusades,
these pilgrimages in the name of the Cross were
the *natural* outcome of the spirit of England in the
days of Richard the First.

.   .   .   .

When Mr. Chesterton talks of Merry England,
he talks of that time in English history which is
known as the Middle Ages.   I have never yet discovered exactly what historians mean by the Middle
Ages   The Middle surely means the centre with
an equal amount on each side.   There is no

equal amount of years on either side of one particular epoch or period of history, for we do not
know yet how long the world will last or for that
matter how long it has lasted. Until we know
these two things definitely how can we asign a
middle to history ? However we must conform
to what is popularly known as the Middle Ages
and say a little of what Mr. Chesterton says about
this era.

Mr. Chesterton is always a little hard on the
historians or those people he so frequently calls
" modern critics." After all there is no greater
modern critic to-day than Mr. Chesterton, and he is
frequently right in what he says ! Mr. Chesterton
is always rather concerned to show that the Middle
Ages were not outrageously cruel. I do not
believe that the defence is needed. Those who
think are perfectly aware that the Middle Ages
cannot be judged successfully by the standards of
our own time.

Mr. Chesterton writes that those who condemned
the policy of the Middle Ages only looked at the
shadows and not at the substance. As a matter of
fact modern critics of that period are much concerned to show that the substance of the Middle
Ages was quite a good substance. The modern
critic is not content with the shadow, the modern
historian may have to be, because the time allotted
at school for history usually only allows for the
shadow.

Again Mr. Chesterton is very zealous that the
Middle Ages are not so bad as they are painted but

do we always believe pictures ?   From what Mr.
Chesterton says, it seems that those who must be
called the dependent classes did not do so badly.
These classes never have done so badly in England,
for the very good reason that a dependent quite
often does not have to have very much upon which
to depend.

Thus he writes of the position of the underlings
under the lords.

" It must be remembered that over a great part,
and especially very important parts, of the whole
territory, the lords were abbots, magistrates elected
by a mystical communism and themselves often
of peasant birth.   Men not only obtained a fair
amount of justice under their care, but a fair
amount of freedom even from their carelessness."

This merely seems to show, that in all ages, the
regime of an autocracy need not be in the least of
the nature of a tyranny.   So the Land Question,
if we can term it such, in the Middle Ages was
moderately satisfactory.

Mr. Chesterton has some very instructive things
to say about those misunderstood Guilds of the
age of Merry England.   Ordinary history surely
shamefully neglects this prominent side of the
Middle Ages.   Mr. Chesterton explains that a
Guild was an organisation after this manner.

" A Guild was, very broadly speaking, a Trade
Union in which every man was his own employer.
That is, a man could not work at any trade unless
he would join the league and accept the laws of
that trade ; but he worked in his own shop with

his own tools and the whole profit went to himself."

It is also of the utmost importance that we should fully understand what was the nature of an employer for it is on this question that so much of the charge of tyranny often originates. The meaning of the word, employer, as Mr. Chesterton makes it quite clear, was something quite different to the modern interpretation of the word. And I conceive that it was a far better and more humanitarian conception.

" A master meant something quite other and greater than a ' boss.' It meant a master of the work, where it now means only a master of the workmen."

Wherefore it may be said with all truth, that in at least this respect, the Middle Ages were better.

There seems to be a very mistaken idea, according to the position of Mr. Chesterton, that government long ago depended upon force of arms. This Mr. Chesterton holds to be a profound error.

" We are told so monotonously that the government of our fathers reposed upon arms, that it is valid to insist that this, their most intimate and everyday sort of government was wholly based upon tools ; a government in which the workman's tool became the sceptre." And the mistaken idea of this government by force and arms instead of by tools or weapons of production and peace may easily have been caused by the fact that, in the name of heraldry productive weapons asssumed heraldry they did not really possess. In this way does Mr. Chesterton make the idea plain.

"The Guilds often exhibited emblems and pageantry so compact of their most prosaic uses, that we can only parallel them by imagining armorial tabards, or even religious vestments, woven out of a navvy's corderoys or a coster's pearl buttons."

To discuss but one more feature of the organisation of the Middle Ages, it is necessary to refer to the Charter.

Mr. Chesterton explains what this really was ; by comparing a Charter to a Trades Union. There is an interesting parallelism between the two, a connecting link between to-day and some hundreds of years ago.

" To recur once more to the parallel of Trades Union as convenient for the casual reader of to-day, the Charter of a Guild roughly corresponded to that ' Recognition ' for which the railwayman and other trades unionists asked some years ago, without success."

And by far the most important part of the Charter, was that it was the germ for something which in our own day is so stable, so taken for granted, that its true nature is not known of the common people. For it was out of the Charter that there grew, that thing about which Mr. Chesterton is always most brilliant, Parliament. In a word this was how Parliament came. Mr. Chesterton puts it clearly and most admirably.

" We should immediately have discovered that England was full of little parliaments, out of which the great parliament was made."

And about this period of Merry England, the time of Guilds and the time of the Charter, Mr. Chesterton ends up with a melancholy statement. For Parliament turned a traitor and destroyed its parents, a horrid form of patricide and matricide. "It is that the Parliament was the one among these mediaeval creations which ultimately consented to betray and to destroy the rest."

But Parliament has not destroyed the Trade Unions, nor, and this is far more important, have the Trade Unions succeeded in destroying Parliament in spite of their well meant, but badly engineered efforts. Parliament cannot be broken from the outside but it may be broken from the inside but the end is not yet, in spite of the pessimism of Mr. Belloc and the warlike threats of the Communists.

Merry England then for Mr. Chesterton was England, a land in which a man could live pretty comfortably, protected by a Guild and cheered by the beginnings of a great and glorious age of learning. We have been prone to think of the Middle Ages as the bad old days, with Mr. Chesterton we may think of them as the *nearly* " good old days."

   .   .   .   .

I have a strong suspicion that there is no person who is so hated to-day as the person who is known as a Puritan. That the popular conception of what a Puritan really was and what is signified by the term to-day, is vastly contradictory, does not matter. Popularly speaking, when people say that a man is a Puritan they mean that he does not bet, that he does not openly express his love of low books and lower people, when people say that a woman is a Puritan they mean that she does not visit night clubs, does not boast of the delights of adultery. Very seldom do modern people realise that Puritanism primarily was (and I contend is), a very definite conception of God. And from this conception of God grew in the seventeenth century the movement which is known as Puritanism.

Now it is very firmly my opinion that Mr. Chesterton knows exactly what the Puritans did stand for, and knowing that, he treats them reasonably. I am equally firmly convinced that modern men and women of the world know nothing at all of what Puritanism was, except that they see it as a colossal and irritating "don't."

It will be well then at once to see exactly what Mr. Chesterton thinks Puritanism did mean or rather what the Puritans stood for. For unless we understand this, it is impossible to get any clear conception of the Age of the Puritans.

" The honest Puritan, growing up in youth in a world swept bare by the great pillage, possessed himself of a first principle which is one of the three or four alternative first principles which are possible to the mind of man. It was the principle that the mind of men can alone directly deal with the mind of God."

In other words, then the Puritan of the seven-

teenth century was a mystic. He considered
that he could get in touch with God without the
necessity of any mediators. I think it ought to
be realised that the primary reason why the
Puritans hated any symbolism in religion, was not
so much that they hated it for its own sake, but
that it developed a line of thinking that would
ultimately result in a reaction from mysticism.
This mysticism quite logically (for the Puritans
were as logical as the Catholics) led to a dislike
of any kind of external approach to God. Mr.
Chesterton describes their religion by " pure feeling,"
in this manner.

" It may shortly be called the anti-sacramental
principle ; but it really applies and he (the Puritan) really applied it to many things besides the
sacraments of the Church. It equally applies
and he equally applied it, to art, to letters, to the
love of locality, to music, and even to good
manners."

A country then that entirely adopted Puritanism would in time destroy much that can so loosely
be called beautiful. The Puritan would not so
much attack or make morality, as attack beauty,
because the mystic in his pure approach to God
cannot make use of the beautiful things or exter-
nals, that the Sacramentalist can use, in *his*
approach to the Deity. It is a curious thing
that mysticism, the attempt to be absorbed (in a
sense) with the Divine Beauty of the Universe,
would by its very method of approach do without
many of the beauties of the material universe.

The spiritual beauty of the mystic or the Puritan may be more excellent than the material beauty of the Sacramentalist, but the material beauty of the Sacramentalist, will be more likely to lead the world to religion, than the austerity and unadorned methods of the Puritans.

The Puritans then tend to introduce an austerity into every form of art but it is unfair to blame them, when we remember their conception of the Deity. It is, on the same grounds equally unfair to condemn the opposite school, the Ritualists, when we consider carefully *their* conception of the Supreme Being.

And there is a subtle attraction in this Puritanism so subtle that it nearly captured seventeenth century England. But, what an escape, says Mr. Chesterton, thank God and thank God that He preferred to be quite obviously approached by others than the Puritans.

There is however to be noted a vast difference in how Puritanism affected England and Scotland.

" Hence in Scotland Puritanism was the main thing, and was mixed with Parliamentary and other oligarchies. In England Parliamentary oligarchy was the main thing and was mixed with Puritanism."

It is interesting to note what exactly Mr. Chesterton thinks was the position of Oliver Cromwell with regard to Puritanism. He was a " taming " influence on the movement or creed.

" Oliver Cromwell is in history much less the leader of Puritanism than the tamer of Puritanism.

He was undoubtedly possessed all his life by the rather sombre religious passions of his period ; but as he emerges into importance, he stands more and more for the Positivism of the English as compared with the Puritanism of the Scotch."

He was in a sense a Puritan but he was really perhaps too tolerant to be a staunch one. Tolerance is quite often the first step to a breach. Church or Creed can depend much more upon its fanatics than upon its tolerant members. If the Catholic Church had been tolerant all through history, it would have probably been reduced to being *a* Church instead of, as she claims, *the* Church. Tolerance is one of the quickest roads very often to total disruption.

In fact Chesterton goes so far as to say that Cromwell killed Charles the First to please some of the more inhuman of the Puritans. Another very good reason for saying, that in a certain degree Cromwell was a protest against much of Puritan sm. This is how Mr. Chesterton puts this question of the beheading of Charles, that spectacle which has given Mr. John Drinkwater one of his finest stage scenes in which his written word is almost entirely silent !

" The act of killing the King, I fancy, was not primarily his, and certainly not characteristically his. It was a concession to the high inhuman ideals of the tiny group of true Puritans with whom he had to compromise but with whom he afterwards collided. It was logic rather than cruelty in the act that was not Cromwellian ; for he treated with bestial cruelty the native Irish, whom the new spiritual exclusiveness regarded as beasts or as the modern euphemism would put it, as aborigines."

So England was in a way rescued from Puritanism.   Mr. Chesterton gives the saving of Christmas as an example.

" Similarly the remains of Christmas were rescued from the Puritans ; but they had eventually to be rescued again by Dickens from the Utilitarians, and may yet have to be rescued by somebody from the vegetarians and the teetotallers."   But ; it is much more likely that Christmas will have to be rescued from the emancipation of the modern woman, for modern woman cannot worship a King born in a Manger, it must worship a King that *might* be born in a Manger but is not born because it has been prevented from birth by Contraception.

The Puritans will never destroy Christmas but modern enlightened and emancipated women are doing their best.   But they will have a hard task to succeed, and when they have destroyed Christmas, they will have destroyed both their souls and bodies, because they will have committed the Sin against the Holy Ghost.

．　　．　　．　　．　　．　　．　　．

In this Essay I have dealt with two religious movements and one political and economic period. The Crusades were characterised by all the pomp and glamour and symbolism that Puritanism so violently repudiated.

The Middle Ages was the age of Guilds and as such was the age that concerned the relationship between master and man.

Mr. Chesterton's approach to history is a somewhat curious one. It is an approach that is characterised by a very rigid dogmatism. Mr. Chesterton is certain of two things. He is certain that the orthodox historians know nothing or very little about the real facts of history. He is equally certain that history, to be properly understood, movements to be viewed in their right perspective, must be viewed through the eyes of Mr. Chesterton !

Mr. Chesterton is always a protest and he is also a symbol. He is a protest against the schoolboy method of teaching history, he is a symbol of what the really literary man does think about the ages that have preceded the one in which he happens to live.

Mr. Chesterton certainly throws new light on history but the question is, does he throw *accurate* light on it ? The historians who do not agree with him will say that his light is new but inaccurate, the public which *does* agree with him will say that he throws both new light and accuracy on to the screen of history.

I am a member of the public and I believe, broadly speaking, that Mr. Chesterton invests history with new qualities and new eventualities and I believe also that his perception leads him to be a more accurate interpreter of the past than many purely dull and professional historians.

END OF PEEP FIVE.

Peep Number Six.

H. G. WELLS AND MARRIAGE.

ON the title page of his book " Marriage "
Mr. Wells quotes the following cynical
observation :
" And the Poor Dears haven't the shadow of a
doubt they will live happily ever afterwards."
This is exactly the reason why so many marriages are a failure, nearly everyone who marries
thinks that his marriage is bound to turn out all
right. Although he may see married misery all
round, the young man full of joy at capturing
some very commonplace girl, thinks that this
commonplace girl is going to be an angel ; when
she turns out to be nothing more or nothing less
than commonplace he is inclined to be disappointed.
The young girl full of joy at the capture she
has made or the capture in which she has been
the willing victim, thinks she has captured Sir
Galahad and then wakes up to find that her
husband is a mere nobody, a bank clerk in some
obscure and delightfully respectable suburb.
But now, and for ever, young people in love,
about to marry, will think that it is going to be

glorious and that like the dear old fairy tale (which may God preserve for ever) they will live happily ever after.

Now every writer of the present day has something to say about marriage. Or rather if that be too outrageously sweeping, let me say that every writer who deals in any way with sociology, considers this vexed question.

There is Shaw writing a clear and forcible treatise on marriage in " Getting Married." There is Chesterton waxing eloquent on marriage, in a book he chooses to call " The Superstition of Divorce." There is Sir James Barrie whimsically concerned with the marriage problem in " Dear Brutus." It is then, only natural, that Mr. Wells should have his say and have his say in a novel.

Of course the amusing part of the whole thing is that no one takes the very faintest real notice of what any of these writers say. And if you ask why, the answer is very simple. It is not that the modern world despises Shaw, or laughs at Chesterton, or disagrees violently, with Barrie. In fact the modern world does not even wish to ignore Wells ! No, the answer is quite simple, so simple that it might be overlooked. This is the answer, the answer why people marry and have married and will marry until the end of time.

" And the Poor Dears haven't the shadow of a doubt they will live happily ever afterwards."

Of course they haven't, the " Poor Dears," but perhaps their optimism is good, even if it ends in a melancholy pessimism. For Love's young dream, is a dear dream while it lasts and sometimes it recurs to cheer the old people who had nearly, but not quite, forgotten. It is a dear dream because it is a dream that is based on the purest of emotions, it is a dear dream because it raises man from the mere animal to something very nearly divine. And even if the drop in after years, is prodigious, even a very faded memory may be better than the bitter cry, that the fairy partnership was never attempted.

.   .   .   .

In this Essay I am attempting to say something about Mr. Well's novel " Marriage." Following the plan of the Essay that I wrote in connection with " Alberta Christina's Father " I shall endeavour to give some idea of what Mr. Wells does feel about marriage. For though as I say, what he feels about it, will not I am sure have the smallest influence on one couple about to be married, this is not to say that the matter is not of some interest to the general public, which for the most part has married and for the most part has not married more unhappily than it probably deserves !

It may as well be discussed at once what is the remedy for an unhappy marriage. According to Mr. Wells, it is a little difficult to accomplish. For you must pack right up, hurry away from your home, leave your friends and relations far away, and embark on a journey that takes you to some detestable foreign clime where comfort is unknown.

There, in such a delectable spot, will you discover
the love that has been lost in the midst of civilisation.   And of course it may be perfectly true
that what Mr .Wells advises is very excellent.   I
have an idea that the bank clerk in Golders Green
who has violent wishes to love the wife of his
neighbour next door may find that the climate of
Greenland induces him to find his own wife quite
worth making love too after all.   I also can
conceive that the purveyor of flaked rice may grow
tired of his virtuous wife in Surbiton and long
for the delights that Regent Street offers, yet I
can conceive this purveyor of flaked rice, madly
in love with his own wife, if there be no other
white woman within fifty miles !

But, this is where Mr. Well's advice falls a little
flat.   The Golders Green bank clerk cannot go to
Greenland to recover his lost love, he may get to
Margate but the probability is that the change will
induce in him the necessity of a change of wives.
So with the Surbiton purveyor of flaked rice,
send him to Brighton and he will grow even more
tired of his wife, but send him to the North West
Frontier and his old love may be regained.   But
then it is not every purveyor of flaked rice who
can go to the North West Frontier.   Unfortunately in
most cases then, Mr. Well's remedy cannot be tried.

Having then determined that Mr. Wells has a
remedy for unhappy marriages, we have further
determined that his remedy, for most people, is
quite unpractical.   So he has not much helped the
marriage problem.   But on " Marriage " he has

created one of his most brilliant books. It is a superb picture of middle class people, those people whose home is a villa but whose outlook extends considerably further.

I say that Mr. Wells has drawn a superb picture of middle class people. Let us follow him when he catches these most estimable people at their evening meal. The Popes, dear good people, have taken a Vicarage. They are at a meal in the evening, Miss Pope, Mr. Well's heroine, is present and her adorer, one Mr. Magnet, a writer of humour. It is kind of Mr. Wells to take us into such a genial atmosphere, quite sincere, the spectacle is one to encourage, for old England thrives on such gatherings.

Mrs. Pope tells us exactly what kind of meal it is. You can see that she says it in that hospitable way, which means to say " I love entertaining people to supper, and especially when one is a writer on humour."

" It's quite a simple farmhouse supper," said Mrs. Pope.

And here is the delightful menu, and oh, Mr. Wells, you have made us hungry to eat and more hungry to be one of this genial company.

" There were ducks, green peas, and adolescent new potatoes for supper, and afterwards stewed fruit and cream and junket and cheese, bottled beer, Gilbey's Burgundy and home-made lemonade. Mrs. Pope carved, because Mr. Pope splashed too much, and bones upset him and made him want to show up chicken in the ' Times.' "

Mr. Magnet the guest of the evening at the farm house supper, is a magnificent creation. You can almost hear Mr. Wells laugh as he created him. I know Mr. Chesterton would roar with a great roaring laugh at the spectacle of the modesty of Mr. Magnet. The naïve way in which he expresses surprise that he is to be the guest of a well known literary club. Then the delicate flattery of Mrs. Pope, for Mr. Magnet has an eye for her daughter. The passage, I quote, I suggest brings out all the Wells humour, the Wells satire, the Wells observation of character, the Wells realism.

" Then Mrs. Pope asked Mr. Wintersloan about his route to Buryhamstreet, and then Mr. Pope asked Mr. Magnet whether he was playing at a new work or working at a new play.

Mr. Magnet said he was dreaming over a play. He wanted to bring out the more serious side of his humour, go a little deeper into things than he had hitherto done.

" Mingling smiles and tears," said Mr. Pope approvingly.

Mr. Magnet said very quietly that all true humour did that.

Then Mrs. Pope asked what the play was to be about and Mr. Magnet, who seemed disinclined to give an answer, turned the subject by saying he had to prepare an address on humour for the next dinner of the *Literati*. " It's to be a humourist's dinner, and they've made me the guest of the evening—by way of a joke he said with that dry smile again."

Mr. Wells then draws Mrs. Pope so admirably. One line only just gives her away, she has ambitions, Mr. Magnet has a name, Mrs. Pope has a daughter !

"Mrs Pope said he shouldn't say things like that."

And later, when the party has been well filled with Gilbey's Burgundy, tongues are loosened, the room rings with the genial merriment of good stories, no matter that they are old, no matter that they may be a little feeble, no matter that the telling of them might be done better, the atmosphere is perfect. Take an English family, fill them, but not too full, with ducks and burgundy, then sit round the table, tell stories, listen to the roars of laughter that go dancing all round the room and you are in home life at its sweetest moment. Mr. Wells catches the atmosphere, a line or two will show this.

"And then for a time the men told stories as they came into their heads in an easy irresponsible way. Mr. Magnet spoke of the humour of the omnibus driver who always dangled and dwiddled his badge ' by way of a joke ' when he passed the conductor whose father had been hanged."

And so on to the inevitable story which no doubt took spots off the ceiling. We can see Mr. Pope hooting with laughter and Mrs. Pope in an ecstasy.

". . . then Mr. Pope reminded them of the heartless husband who, suddenly informed that his mother-in-law was dead exclaimed, ' oh don't make me laugh please, I've got a split lip . . .' "

In the case of the problem as to whether it is probable that Marjorie Pope would have become engaged to Mr. Magnet, we are face to face with something that I shall call the choice of the alternative. In this way. If Marjorie did not engage herself to Mr. Magnet, she had in prospect this kind of environment. I have already said that Mr. Wells is superb in the creation of middle class people. I have shown how admirably he shows how they behave at dinner. Let us go to the other extreme, Mr. Pope, no longer filled with Gilbey's Burgundy, no longer the genial host at an ample " farmhouse supper," but the disgruntled head of the family at breakfast, that awful meal which is the real England at its dreariest.

Here then is the alternative, if Marjorie does not get engaged to Magnet, an unending vista of these domestic battles.

" Her father was ' horrid ' at breakfast."

And marriage might get her away. If not :

" And very soon she would have to come home and live in the midst of this again—indefinitely." How many women see this possibility and instead choose a husband who will at least save them from the boring life as a daughter at home ? "

It is perhaps somewhat cynical to suggest that quite often the alternative is the choice of two evils, but I believe it is a truism.

With the alternative in view of life at home or life with Mr. Magnet, I do not think that Mr. Wells strays beyond the bounds of probability by making Marjorie accept Mr. Magnet. With grim realism Mr. Wells gives us a picture of the feminine drivel that Marjorie indulges in at her proposal. It is the sickening tripe that every young man loves to hear, for the words are not " tripe " to him but precious gold exuding from the lips of an angel.

" I don't think I knew what I meant," said Marjorie, and Magnet gave a queer sound of relief at her words. I don't think I know what I mean now. I don't think I can say I love you, Mr. Magnet. I would if I could. I like you very much indeed, I think you are awfully kind, you're more kind and generous than any one I have ever known."

Marjorie than asks one of those futile questions that women like to ask. There is no conceivable rational answer which is precisely the reason that the question is asked. Of course poor dear Magnet cannot understand.

" I wonder," she said, " if you can understand what it is to be a girl ? "

If wives could understand what it is to be a husband or husbands understand what it is to be a wife, it is quite conceivable that the divorce courts would find themselves less popular than they are. But I do not think that we can ever tell what it would be like to be another sex. We may think we know, but we only know in so far as we *imagine* ourselves to be something else. Unless we could change our sex in actuality, it is I conceive, impossible to know what state of feeling towards life the change would involve. If we could change our sex perhaps we should be gods indeed, perhaps God is both sexes, which is a good reason for suggesting that He is Perfect Understanding.

But to revert to Mr. Magnet.

In creating this character Mr. Wells has written of a self-satisfied prig. A man that any woman would do well to avoid, unless she could smack him soundly and frequently.

Mr. Magnet's odious self satisfaction is shown in his behaviour after he has addressed the members of the *Literati*. No wonder Marjorie is a little disgusted at his complacency but I believe that most women dislike men who are very pleased with themselves. Women much prefer it that men should be pleased with them.

" Mr. Magnet arrived by the 2.27, and to Marjorie's eye his alighting presence had an effect of being not so much covered with laurels as distended by them. His face seemed whiter and larger than ever. He waved a great handful of newspapers."

His words indicate only too well that he would not only be a husband who was interested in himself but he would expect his wife to be interested in him also. So many men seem to imagine that every little thing they do must of course be of the intensest interest to their wives, they appear to forget that even in marriage women do not change their sex or their interests. Besides, a wife does not care only to be used as a kind of instrument for a husband to derive flattery from. Most women would be annoyed at the complacency of Magnet and particularly in our own day of emancipated woman.

Mr. Wells draws Mr. Magnet's unbounded self assertion cleverly. Only too well does he know the conceit of the literary man who has been the guest of the evening and thinks that he is the guest of the whole universe.

" ' Hullo ! Magsy ! ' he said. ' They've given me a thumping Press, I'm nearer swelled head than I've ever been, so mind how you touch me ! ' "

To which Marjorie (we will not be so vulgar as to call her " Magsy ") replies with true feminine pragmatism.

" We'll take it down at croquet."

Almost as an afterthought Magnet makes an attempt to kiss Marjorie. It is skilful character delineation. Mr. Wells knows that if you are to capture a woman, and Marjorie had to be captured, it is necessary to kiss her first, it must never be an afterthought. Kiss first and then show the press cuttings is far wiser than showing the press cuttings first and kissing after.

And soon after this episode Mr. Wells makes Marjorie fall in love with a man who fell from the sky, and now leaving the unfortunate Mr. Magnet to his press cuttings and his regrets we must say something ot Marjorie Pope when she has become Marjorie Trafford.

.   .   .   .

It is so seldom that Mr. Wells indulges in a beautiful piece of writing that it is pleasant to be

able to refer to it. When I say beautiful I mean
the type of writing that has something to do with
wistfulness and human nature at its best. It
concerns the time of the honeymoon of Marjorie
Trafford and she and her husband have met an
old peasant pair in sweet Italy. Dear old people,
these peasants, dwelling on the tops of the mountain
ranges, very near to God, they seem to derive
something of the beauty of heaven in their beings.

The old man sees the happy young couple.
The sight makes him say this beautiful saying.
There is a wealth of good nature in the remark.

" Isn't it good dear, to think that once you and
I may have looked like that to some passer-by.
I wish I could bless them—sweet swift young
things ! I wish, dear, it was possible for old men
to bless young people without seeming to set up
for saint . . . ."

But the old people need not think that young
people mind a blessing from those who are old.
Young people mind nothing when they are on a
honeymoon but perhaps they need no blessing
then, but the blessing of old people lingers when
the dream days of the honeymoon have turned to
the realities of marriage.

No, the old need not think that the young resent
a blessing when it is given in sincerity and none are
so sincere as those who dwell in the quiet solitudes
of the country in the places where the great storms
sweep down, in the remote intimacy with nature
which so often creates a fine understanding of
mankind.

But I must, alas, hurry on far beyond the days of the honeymoon, far away from the divinities of Italy, far away into a marriage controversy. And the controversy that Mr. Wells introduces is unfortunately a common one. It concerns the difficult question of the husband who puts his work before his wife. And to succeed, I suggest that this is quite necessary, for work absorbs all the attention at the time, even so much, that a wife may well feel neglected. Mr. Wells puts the problem into some realistic dialogue, the kind of dialogue that appears to be so common to marriage, when the first esctasies have passed so swiftly away, that they are almost forgotten.

"You see," he said on his knees, " I'd really got hold of my work at last."

"But you should have sent—— "

"I was thinking of my work. I clean forgot."

"Forgot ? "

"Absolutely."

"Forgot——me ! "

"Of course," said Trafford, with a slightly puzzled air ; "you don't see it as I do."

That is just the unpleasant point. It is so seldom that a wife sees her husband must appear at times to neglect her in favour of his work. Fond, as no doubt, Trafford was of his wife, this fondness, as Mr. Wells indicates, did not prevent him at times from absolute absorption in his work. And Marjorie being but ordinary (she cannot be blamed) feels naturally hurt, a woman wants to come first and what is more she wants her husband

to continually remind her of this fact. So Mr.
Wells introduces us to this little misunderstanding,
but little misunderstandings in marriage are really
very big, for they are the milestones on the road
that can lead so rapidly and so inevitably to dis-
illusion and matrimonial unhappiness. And it is
not easy to say who is to blame, for I contend most
earnestly that marriage does not change people
in their *essentials*. The man still puts his work
first ; the woman still wants to take priority to all
else.

And a little later, Mr. Wells becomes quite
philosophical over the question of marriage. He
philosophises about that difficult period of marriage
when there is no longer any element of surprise
left. I think that Mr. Well's words are so wise
and so sympathetic that a quotation of some
length will indicate his position clearly.

" And now indeed, the Traffords were coming
to the most difficult and fatal phase in marriage.
They had had that taste of defiant adventure
which is the crown of a spirited love affair, they
had known the sweetness of a maiden passion for a
maid, and they had felt all those rich and solemn
emotions, those splendid fears and terrible hopes
that weave themselves about the great partnership
in parentage."

That is the beginning, we now arrive, not at the
end, but in the still water when all the passion and
excitement have passed, when it will be proved
whether the partnership is a real one or a mere
transitory attachment that cannot survive the

withdrawal of all mystery and the fulfilment of all desire. I am afraid that Mr. Wells is a little pessimistic.

He writes thus :

" And now, so far as sex was concerned, there might be much joy and delight still, but no more wonder, no fresh discoveries of incredible new worlds and unsuspected stars. Love, which had been a new garden, an unknown land, a sunlit sea to launch upon, was now a rich treasure house of memories. And memories, although they afford a perpetually increasing enrichment to emotion, are not sufficient in themselves for the daily needs of life. For this, indeed, is the truth of passionate love, that it works out its purpose and comes to an end."

So far Mr. Wells is right. But true love survives the end of passion and rather than feeling the loss of it, takes to itself a far grander emotion, that of trust and infinite understanding. But such marriages are are.

" A day arrives in every marriage when the lovers must face each other, disillusioned, stripped of the last shred of excitement—undisguisedly themselves."

And this was what had happened to Marjorie Trafford and her husband. And Trafford had experienced the most terrible blow of all—his wife was not what she had seemed, she was commonplace—and he had sacrificed his work for her. Mr. Wells does not shirk the miserable position, a far more miserable position than to find that the other party has been unfaithful.

" He had crippled, he perceived more and more clearly, the research work upon which his whole being had once been set, and his hours were full of tiresome and trivial duties and his mind engaged and worried by growing financial anxieties."

And all for a woman who was not quite what he had thought her to be. And, make no mistake, it was not the fault of Marjorie, nor was it the fault of Trafford. It was just that sad thing, that love blinds and we cannot see where we go, we are blinded by the brilliance of the glorious sun and then all at once it is dark, the glare has dazzled our eyes, then again the darkness lifts, but it displays no longer the fierce sunlight, but things as they really are. And it is again so sad, the things as they really are, are not what we had wanted and the awakening is a desperate anguish. So poor Trafford wakes up and sees Marjorie and his child just as they are, very commonplace and perhaps, hardly worth the sacrifice of his work.

" He had made these abandonments in a phase of exalted passion, for the one woman in the world and her unprecedented child, and now he saw, in spite of all his desire not to see, that she was just a weak human being among human beings, and neither she nor little Margharita so very marvellous."

Then Mr. Wells most skilfully compares the ever increasing excitement of scientific research with the deadening finish to the adventures of passionate love. For in science there are always new fields to conquer, new discoveries to be made, but in marriage when the fatal period has been reached, the terminus has been reached, there are no fresh fields, there is the boundary and it cannot be extended.

" But while Marjorie shrank to the dimensions of reality, research remained still a luminous and commanding dream. In love one fails or one wins home. but the lure of research is for ever beyond the hills, every victory is a new desire. Science has inexhaustively fresh worlds to conquer . . ."

.   .   .   .

I think that it is true to say that the general conclusion of Mr. Wells comes to in " Marriage " is that there is a danger of it becoming dull. It is fair to deduce this general principle from the example of the Traffords. Mr. Wells of course tries the experiment of sending them to a far and foreign clime, and they recover their lost love. But as the number of people who can try this experiment is very strictly limited, Mr. Wells, as I have said, gives us no remedy.

With regard to the probability of the book. It has been argued that Marjorie would not have been likely to let herself become engaged to Magnet. I have attempted to prove such a supposition wrong by a discussion of the problem of *alternative* that faces many girls and faced Marjorie Pope.

That Marjorie would have fallen violently in love with Trafford seems to be perfectly reasonable. That he would get tired of her and long for the opportunity of giving all his attention to his work, seems to me, to be equally reasonable.

It may be no part of this Essay to suggest a way that marriages may be made more happy for a greater number of people. But it may be suggested that there would be more happy marriages if people did not expect so much out of the matrimonial contract. Mr. Wells shows us how much Trafford expected from his marriage and—he was disappointed.

But as I said at the beginning, whatever writers may like to write, however much they may like to advise, however much they may warn, few, if any, will take any notice of what they say. For each about to be married couple thinks their case to be unique, " poor old Wells," they say, " what does he know about our wonderful love the like of which the world has never seen before ? " " Shaw, Chesterton," did you say, " but they mean about other marriages, they do not refer to *our* coming glorious life."

No, they will not listen, these dear young people caught up in the ecstacy of their new found wonder, no, they have no gift of prophesy, the road seems to lead to a golden city and . . . " the Poor Dears haven't the shadow of a doubt they will live happily ever afterwards."

END OF PEEP SIX.

JACK LONDON AND THE UNEXPECTED.

ONE day, not so very long ago, the morning papers announced with all their baldness, that Jack London had died. And, we who loved the grim realism and deep understanding of his books, realised that a writer of hurricane force had passed from the earth and the earth was the poorer for his passing. For Jack London was one of those writers who combined a very sound common sense with an extraordinary power of writing terrific melodrama. London understood life and he could write of its frantic struggles, its delicious romance and its startling, terrifying mystery and tragedy. London wrote with a pen that literally galloped and the galloping left the reader gasping for breath and yet eager to read on, even if the reading became almost a painful emotion.

In this Essay, I have taken one of Jack London's short stories and I have taken that remarkable tale which he called " The Unexpected." By an examination of this something can be seen of the philosophy of this melodramatic and brilliant man of literary thrills. For that is exactly what

London was, a literary man who could thrill *par excellence*.

. . . .

It is one of the most interesting things in the world to watch the effect of something that is unexpected on an individual. The unexpected may bring out the best qualities in an individual, it may quite equally bring out the worst. A man may go to the City every morning, he may return every evening and become so accustomed to seeing his wife ready to meet him at the evening dinner, that he conceives that she is as certain to be there, as the sun is certain to rise on the following morning. Then, one evening he returns as usual, the house still stands in the little suburban road, the boys still ride down the road on their way to tennis, the 6.40, has as usual, just roared its way into the tunnel, but on his return to the house, the city man finds that his wife has died very suddenly, a fainting fit, an attempted revival by brandy and all is over. It is the unexpected, it will induce in that city man a new outlook on life. He will acquire adaptability by the sudden violent application of the unexpected on the one hand, or on the other hand, he may be suddenly thrown off his mental balance with a subsequent violent reversal of all his principles and ideals.

It is with the result of the unexpected on two people, that Mr. London deals in his story " The Unexepcted." Mr. London is of the opinion that the application of the unexpected in life is a kind of test, the unexpected selects and it knows whom it will beat and by whom it will be beaten. This is the way in which Mr. London puts his proposition.

"When the unexpected does happen, however, and when it is of sufficiently grave import, the unfit perish. They do not see what is not obvious, are unable to do the unexpected, are incapable of adjusting their well-groomed lives to other and strange grooves. In short, when they come to the end of their own groove, they die."

I think that it may be wise, in so far as it goes, to accept what Mr. London postulates. But I am very firmly convinced that a very large number of people are perfectly able to adapt themselves to meet a progress of events that they had not thought about. The concrete example is the great war, that dastardly outrage which showed us that millions of men and women were quite able to adapt themselves to Hell, when they had been living lives, not in Heaven, but on earth in very ordinary and orthodox days. But it is perfectly true to say that those who cannot meet the unexpected die, for if they do not die physically, they die mentally and spiritually. Mr. London, in the story that I am writing about, deals with a woman who was able to meet the unexpected when it was thrust upon her in the most violent and dreadful way that it is possible to imagine. Any event which Jack London writes of, if it is at all dramatic, may be quite certain to be drama to he last degree.

And let us look at the chief character of this remarkable story, the type of woman that Mr. London thinks can withstand the onslaught of the unexpected. She is one ; Edith Whittlesey and she is one of those women who will never be beaten because she is never smashed by the most terrific reversal of her fortunes.

" She was born in a rural district of England, where life proceeds by rule of thumb and the unexpected is so very unexpected that when it happens it is looked upon as an immorality."

Yet in spite of this Mr. London tells us that Edith was one of :

" Those that make toward survival, the fit individuals who escape from the rule of the obvious and the expected and adjust their lives to no matter what strange grooves they may stray into or into which they may be forced."

Then when Edith Whittlesey became Edith Nelson came the sudden rush of the unexpected, the sudden rush that swept away lives, the sudden rush that made madness draw near, the sudden rush that veiled the face of the sun, the sudden rush that made all dark and fearful and full of frightful eventualities and still more frightful possibilities.

But I am anticipating, I must not describe the coming of the actual unexpected to Edith Nelson for a little. I must describe their background so that we can *see* this wonderful woman that Jack London has created, as well as read about her. Edith Nelson found herself one of a gold mining rush that tore away to the fastnesses of Alaska. And here in Alaska in a little wooden cabin dwelt Edith and her husband. And it was the duty of Edith to see to the cabin for you must know that no matter where your home be in Park Lane or in the heart of Alaska, a woman must be there if you would have your home, to be the blessed place that name imp.ies. And it seemed as if life would move evenly, no untoward events, for if you are in a rough country you expect roughess, but the roughness is expected and so it does not hurt so much.

Here is the delightful picture that Mr. London gives when all is prosperous, all content, success and good fellowship.

" There was no grumbling, no bickering, nor petty quarelling in the little cabin and they often congratulated one another on the general happiness of the party. Hans Nelson was stolid and easy going, while Edith had long before won his unbounded admiration by her capacity for getting on with people."

Not a situation in which it might be expected that a dreadful tragedy only waited its evil opportunity to pounce. Perhaps evil is even more clever than we think, for it seems to wait until no one gives it even a passing thought, then suddenly like a vulture, it swoops, it cuts with a two edged sword and withdraws laughing at the bloody havoc it has created.

And now Mr. London swerves right into the drama. The curtain is raised, the eyes strain that

they may see the fearful spectacle, the flesh
creeps, the storm has broken and the lightning
reveals a terrible scene. Tersely does Mr. London
introduce us to the awful tragedy that is about to
take place in that little cabin of happy and successful
people.

"And then the unexpected happened. They
had just sat down to the breakfast table."

A time when you would least expect tragedy,
men well cheered by ample sleep, well filled by
the delights of the table, with the prospect of a
prosperous day's work in front. There is only
the Irishman absent and such is the merriness
of the party that they are laughing at the absence
of Dennin. The dialogue is true of the careless
chat of men with the combination of wanted
food and anticipation of coming success to add
to success already gained. I give a line or two
which is in Mr. London's easy and familiar
style.

" He was never late at meal times before,"
she remarked.

" I cannot understand," said Hans. " Always
had he the great appetite like the horse."

" It is too bad," Dutchy said with a shake of
his head.

They were beginning to make merry over their
comrade's absence.

The merriment went on, still the absent one did
not come in. " They burst into loud laughter
at Dutchy's nonsense."

And then in came the absent member :

" The sound had scarcely died away when the door opened and Dennin came in. All turned to look at him. He was carrying a shot-gun. Even as they looked, he lifted it to his shoulder and fired twice. At the first shot Dutchy sank upon the table overturning his mug of coffee, his yellow mop of hair dabblin in his plate of mush. His forehead, which pressed upon the near edge of the plate, tilted the plate up against his hair at an angle of forty-five degrees. Harkey was in the air in his spring to his feet, at the second shot, and he pitched face down upon the floor, his " My God ! " gurgling and dying in his throat."

This frightful scene was, in the most dramatic sense, something to cause terror. Mr. London merely remarks :

" It was the unexpected."

The effect on Edth and Hans was one of paralysis. The most usual first effect of a very sudden experience of the unexpected, is a sense of paralysis, the brain cannot so suddenly leave an old path and enter on a new one. In Mr. London's story, the brain of Edith has to suddenly adapt itself to a situation of sudden death from the immediate forerunning laughter at a genial meal. At first the transition is too violent to be coped with.

" Hans and Edith were stunned. They sat at the table with bodies tense, their eyes fixed in a fascinated gaze upon the murderer."

But the stunning effect of the murder does not last very long, the instinct for self preservation

arouses the sense of adaptability in Edith. Thus
Mr. London demonstrates a very well attested
truth. Nothing rouses so much from any great
shock as the appearance of danger to ourselves.
Mankind is naturally selfish and naturally desirous
to save itself from premature extinction. And
Edith knew that Dennin meant to kill her and
her husband, so she " recovers " fr m the unexpected.

" For a space of possibly three seconds of time
she had been dazed and paralysed by the horrible
and inconceivable form in which the unexpected
had made its appearance. Then she rose to it and
grappled with it."

In the case then of Edith Nelson, the unexpected
has the effect of making her equal very quickly to
even the most horrible form of tragedy. Death
in its hideous entirety is literally hurled at her in a
moment of time. But, in another moment she
is able to face and contend with the appalling situation. It has now to be shown in the remainder
of this Essay how Mr. London makes Edith
show herself possessed of great determination
and given greater strength rather than any weakness by the coming of the unexpected in the form
of a brutal murder. Mr. London's psychology
seems very sound.

.   .   .   .

In a sense Edith Nelson had the best opportunity possible of recovering from the effects
of the unexpected. The instantaneous action

demanded would restore her balance of mind at once. Mr. London says that certain people do not recover from the onslaught of the unexpected and die. I have already said that I believe this to be true. But quite likely the reason that these people do not recover, in many cases, is that there is really no instant need for them to do so. In the case of the city man I quoted who suddenly found that his wife had died while he was absent at his work in the city. There would be no pressing need to recover from the shock at once. But in the case of Edith Nelson, if she had not recovered immediately, a bullet would have been fired at her and then one for her husband. So she was *forced* to pull herself together. But I do not wish to say from this that I think Mr. London means us to infer that Edith only recovered from the unexpected because of dire necessity, I believe he means Edith to be a type who would be able to fall in line with life however startling its course might be. In the case of her husband, Mr. London makes him to be a little slower in regaining his mental balance. Perhaps a man always takes longer because it takes more to preciptate him into the realms of shock.

" Hans Nelson was half a second behind his wife in rising to the unexpected. His nerve processes and mental processes were slower than hers. His was the grosser organism and it had taken him half a second longer to perceive and to determine and proceed to do."

And the effect again on the two is well brought

out. The woman is cool but the man is near to madness. Blind rage has possessed him but calm determination has invaded the woman. Very skilfully does Mr. London bring out this essential difference in their temperaments. The rage of Hans is so frightful that Edith can hardly believe that it is her husband.

" She could not believe that this raging beast was her Hans and with a shock she became suddenly aware of a shrinking instinctive fear that he might snap her hand in his teeth like any wild animal."

Suddenly through such a small event they find that they are in a new world. A mere plate falling off the table. How well does Mr. London follow the extraordinary thing that we call life.

" The clang of the plate had aroused them to life in a new world. The cabin epitomized the new world in which they must henceforth live and move. The old cabin was gone for ever."

Dreadful words " for ever " ; no matter that we shriek, it can never be the same again, no matter that we threaten, it can never be the same again, no matter that we say that we will kill God, it can never be the same again, then the God that we would have killed if we could, is the God that we thank, that if it can never be the same again, we can in time adapt ourselves to the new conditions.

" The unexpected had swept its wizardy over the face of things, changing the perspective, juggling values, and shuffling the real and the unreal into perplexing confusion."

Then Mr. London gives us a bit of real horror. It is so funny! let us howl with laughter, the breakfast isn't cleared away, the coffee hasn't been finished, the genial dear fellows round the table may want a second helping. And Hans is going outside. His wife asks him why he is going. " To dig some graves."

That is why we laugh ; that still form on the bed, the half empty medicine bottles, the sunlight that comes creeping into the room. What is that noise ? That noise of shovelling, someone is digging a grave, poor fools and we think the world and all its pomp matters one iota. For the man on the bed, the shovelling is going on. Mr. London has finished that breakfast, there is the persistent noice of shovelling graves, and a wasted cup of coffee !

.   .   .   .

The trend of the story of " The Unexpected " is that Dennin the murderer lives and is kept captive in the Nelson's cabin. Mr. London uses a great deal of sound psychology in telling this great drama. It would be difficult to imagine a more curious situation than that depicted by Mr. London. There is the cabin, there is the frozen waste of Alaska, there is the murderer, there are the man and the woman, each having to guard the murderer by turns. The situation again demonstrates how different in every conceivable circumstance is the viewpoint of a man and the viewpoint of a woman. There is something that is almost an antagonism between Edith and her husband. Hans Nelson is obsessed by the idea that it is his duty to kill Dennin ; Edith on the other hand " contended there was only one way to punish Dennin, and that was the legal way arranged by society."

It needs no imagination to conceive of the desperate horror of that hut, the trapped murderer, the husband full of the lust for blood and always just on the border line which separates madness from sanity. Here is a grim picture of Edith on guard lest the prisoner might attempt to escape or attempt to murder his captors.

" So Edith Nelson went back to the terrible cabin with its endless alternating four-hour watches. Sometimes, when it was her turn and she sat by the prisoner, the loaded shot gun in her lap, her eyes would close and she would doze. Always she aroused with a start, snatching up the gun and swiftly looking at him. These were distinct nervous shocks and their effect was not good on her. Such was her fear of the man that, even though she were wide awake, if he moved under the bed clothes, she could not repress the start and the quick reach for the gun."

This was how the woman was affected. Mr. London shows how her determination, her obstinacy, her doggedness prevented her from breaking down. But the sudden and terrific call of the unexpected, the shattering shots and the death cry of the man, made a naturally strong woman far more strong, the unexpected far from beating her had caused her to be the magnificent victor over herself. But the situation affected the man in a different manner. Mr. London brings it out with considerable skill. Hans was quite near to insanity, Edith was probably never more sane, that was the effect of a great shock on two different kinds of people, different in temperament and different in sex.

" Hans was affected differently. He became obsessed by the idea that it was his duty to kill Dennin ; and whenever he waited upon the bound man or watched by him, Edith was troubled by the fear that Hans would add another red story to the cabin's record. Always he cursed Dennin savagely and handled him roughly. Hans tried to conceal his homicidal mania and he would say to his wife, " By and by you will want me to kill him and then I will not kill him. It would make me sick."

And yet, it is the woman who all the time keeps her husband from killing Dennin from making himself a self-appointed judge, woman is the life giver and she is the life preserver, even a brutal murderer cannot let her lose her essential womanhood. But once let a woman lose that and become possessed of a lust for blood and she will cry and crave for blood and demand that it shall surround her on every side. But by then a woman is mad, the women of the French Revolution were mad and as mad as mad dogs, but Edith was not mad. So she will not let her husband suddenly raise his gun and send the brains of Dennin splashing against the cabin wall. " But more than once, stealing into the room when it was her watch off, she would catch the two men glaring ferociously at each other, wild animals the pair of them, in Han's face the lust to kill, in Dennin's the fierceness and savagery of the cornered rat. " Hans," she would cry, " wake up " ! and he would come to a recollection of himself, startled and shamefaced and unrepentant."

The situation in the cabin was obviously one that could not go on indefinitely, so Mr. London introduces a very skilful arrangement for getting rid of Dennin. His solution of the difficulty opens up the very interesting consideration of what really constitutes the law. Something tells Edith that Dennin must not be killed without some kind of trial. Who is to try Dennin ? We are not in England but in the wastes of Alaska. It is the position perhaps of " The Book of Judges." It is the time when it must be that " every man did that which was right in his own eyes." The law of the primitive, if you will, but a law of necessity. Dennin must be got rid of, he could not be allowed to escape, he would take the first opportunity of killing his captors. Mr. London decides that there shall be a tribunal. The woman, quicker witted when a great decision has to be made and especially when the man's reasoning powers are overwhelmed by an intense and obsessing hatred. This is how Mr. London tells us that the idea of a tribunal worked itself out, in the mind of Edith Nelson.

" It came to her that the law was nothing more than the judgement and the will of any group of people. It mattered not how large was the group of people. There were little groups she reasoned, like Switzerland, and there were big groups like the United States. Also, she reasoned, it did not matter how small was the group of people. There might be only ten thousand people in a country yet their collective judgment and will would be the law of that country. Why, then, could not one thousand people constitute such a group, she asked herself. And if one thousand, why not one hundred ? Why not fifty ? Why not five ? Why not—two ? "

It is nearly always the same, we can quite easily argue to our own satisfaction. So the cabin resolved itself into a court of law, the man and his wife were the jury and judge and sentence is passed that Dennin shall be hanged. A very logical and happy conclusion, justice in a rough cabin. Mr. London is able to be quite certain that no matter what are the conditions, justice is seldom entirely ignored. It is the working of the white man's law.

" But the Indians remained solemnly to watch the working of the white man's law that compelled a man to dance upon the air."

.   .   .   .

Whether the events in Mr. London's story : " The Unexpected " are credible is a question with which I am not concerned. In this tale there is a profound study of psychology. The effect of a frightful shock is shown on two people. The two people are a man and a woman and in most ways the woman comes out best.

Mr. London shows by this story that certain people can grapple with and beat any situation, however terrifying, however strained. There seems to be practically no limit to human endurance. Edith and Hans Nelson undergo an ordeal that would have shaken the strongest nerve. Yet they win through. Mr. London loves to write of rough justice, he loves the atmosphere of the log cabin. With the greatest possible skill he introduces his dramatic event and as a sequel almost, he studies pretty minutely the effect of the unexpected on a married couple. If it is interesting to merely mention the *morality* of the story, there might be some controversy as to whether Edith and Hans were right in " trying " Dennin and executing him. In any case the background of the story has to be remembered. It is true that there should not be one law for the rich and one law for the poor, but it should not be forgotten that the law may have to be administered in a crude manner, when the environment is rude.

Perhaps in some ways the obvious thing to have done would have been to shoot Dennin at once and the defence that it was done in self defence would seem to be quite an adequate one. But the way in which the Nelson's behaved was a nobler one, it called forth infinite endurance and infinite restraint. For, if Jack London's story is a story of how the unexpected was contended with, it is also a story of a great restraint. It is further the story of a struggle, a struggle between the restraint of the woman and the impetuous violence of the man. And again the story is a great tribute to women, for the woman comes out best, she is restrained, in a frightful situation she keeps her sanity and she carries through her dreadful task to its logical and appointed finish. If that which is written by Jack London in this story is horror, what is not written, if we use any imagination, is made up of far greater horror. Imagine feeding a man who has killed your two best friends, imagine " nursing " a man who looks at you with eyes that blaze with a hatred that cannot be defined. Imagine the situation for a delicate woman. The horror of the unwritten is greater than the horror of the written. Mr. London is always a grim realist but he is also a philosopher. In the tale that Mr. London has written of the unexpected, he has given a combination of drama, deep psychology and grim horror.

" The Unexpected " is worth reading and it is worth thinking about and the thinking leads very far down into the complex thing that is human nature.

END OF PEEP SEVEN.

STEPHEN LEACOCK AND ENGLAND.

IN this Essay concerning Mr. Leacock I am attempting a twofold task. I want to show something of his humour and I want to say a little about his more serious side, though I am well aware that humour is one of the most serious things in the world, And the world takes Mr. Leacock so seriously that it does not always realise that there is another side to this Professor. And if the humour of Mr. Leacock is serious, his seriousness is also serious ! If it be asked at once, why is Mr. Leacock humourous, I should say that the answer is that he is humourous because he enjoys the life he has been thrown into. His humour is perhaps more than anything else keen observation, his seriousness is also the result of observation.

I have thought it wise as the length of an Essay is necessarily limited, to deal with four themes of the book that Mr. Leacock has called " My Discovery of England." The four themes that I propose to discuss are what Mr. Leacock thinks about London, his attitude to our politics, his

discussion about the British and American Press
and the question of the English and a sense of
humour.

.   .   .   .

Soon after his arrival in London Mr. Leacock
seems to have been much worried by the strange
emotions that the City undergoes. He is not quite
sure what the City really is. " I am still unable
to decide whether the city is a prison, or a place
or a thing." It would be grievous to think that
Mr. Leacock should not know. The City of London
is not a person, a place or a thing, it is a combination of all three, in other words it is a brain !
It works very hard indeed that the other parts of
London may play very hard. But in spite of its
hard work, its head people can consume plenty
of cocktails and its underlings tea and new bath
buns.

Mr. Leacock cannot help indulging in a kind
of mild gibe at the ignorance of the Londoner of
his own town. But he admits that in this respect
the Londoner is not by any means unique, even the
Americans are not without reproach.

" But the Londoners, after all, in not seeing
their own wonders, are only like the rest of the
world. The people who live in Buffalo never go
to see the Niagara Falls ; people in Cleveland
don't know which is Mr. Rockefeller's house ; and
people live and even die in New York without
going up to the top of the Woolworth Building."

But none of these very superior people who

sneer at the fact that the native does not know his own native place seem to be aware that the reason for this ignorance is an astonishingly good one. The Londoner has very little chance of seeing London for the very good reason that while there, work and sleep sap most of his energies. It becomes then a truism that those who know a city best are those who come to visit it as visitors.

Mr. Leacock has an amusing hit at the calm way in which we say that the sun so seldom shines in London, why this is quite untrue says the professor, he has with his own eyes seen the sun shine and no doubt saw that it was very good. This is how he refutes the absurd notion that there is no sun in London during the winter.

" The notion that no sunlight ever gets through and that in the London winter people never see the sun is of course a ridiculous error, circulated by the jealousy of foreign nations."

He then goes on to say that he has personal experience of seeing the sun. And no doubt the sun has been pleased to have been noticed by Mr. Leacock !

" I have myself seen the sun plainly visible in London, without the aid of glasses, on a November day in broad daylight and again one night about four o'clock in the afternoon I saw the sun distinctly appear through the clouds."

Going somewhat into that vague multiplicity in a unity which may be well be called the mind of London, Mr, Leacock found that it was in some ways strangely like New York, at least from an intelligent study of the newspapers of both cities he found a parallel between them. Naturally he would, a few thousands miles of sea water make very little difference to the mind that is fed on the newspaper, the mind that gets its gleanings from the press. There is a parallel in the mind of London and the mind of New York. I will put it down here in the manner that Mr. Leacock does in his book. It seems that indeed London and New York are both two minds with a single thought.

THE MIND OF NEW YORK.	THE MIND OF LONDON.
What is it thinking ?	*What is it thinking ?*
1. Do chorus girls make good wives ?	1. Do chorus girls marry well ?
2. Is fat a sign of genius ?	2. Is genius a sign of fat ? "

In London Mr. Leacock could not escape meeting some of the prominent people, those who emanated from and segregate in certain parts of the Metropolis. He was evidently disappointed in the conversations. But after all even *literary men* must sometimes be ordinary. This was his remembrance of talk with three eminent persons.

" Sir James Barrie said, ' This is really very exceptional weather for this time of year.' "

" Cyril Maude said, ' And so a Martini cocktail is merely gin and vermouth.' "

" Ian Hay " said " You'll find the underground ever so handy once you understand it."

But as these three would hardly dare to be funny in front of a humourist and they would not wish to be tragic, it stands to reason that the commonplace of our enlightened civilisation would be all that was left.

Mr. Leacock gets humour out of his impressions of London because he does not look for humour. He sees it for the very good reason that it needs no looking for. The humour of London is perhaps best seen by the man who is the guest of the great town, for London is gentle to the visitor and gentleness is often humourous or at least it makes the recipient contented and in the mood to appreciate anything funny that may come along. I must now consider Mr. Leacock when he is humourous in a " serious " way and it is with the game of politics.

.   .   .   .   .   .

It is I suppose only natural that in writing something about the politics of England, Mr. Leacock should say something about the Monarchy. Many quite nice people do this, Hyde Park has a lot to say about the king, and it has a lot more it would say if it dared. Now I am not quite sure whether Mr. Leacock really means that he thinks the King's person is too much guarded, that the head of the Royal House is too exclusive. He hankers after Canada where it had been planned to give a Prince of the Blood a tea in the " basement of the Presbyterian Church."

But this is where I am not sure whether Mr. Leacock is humourous and serious or merely serious. As I said at the beginning of this Essay Mr. Leacock is two fold, something in a sense like Barrie and Maconnachie. Anyhow this is what he writes of our dignity of royalty.

" But you don't get that sort of thing in England. There's a formality and coldness in all their dealings with royalty that would never go down with us."

This is I am sure serious. The colonies would not understand our great respect of persons, or rather our elaborate attempts to prove by various gestures, that respect we do feel for the crowned house.

" They like to have the King come and open Parliament dressed in royal robes and with a clattering troop of soldiers riding in front of him."

What I really think Mr. Leacock wants to get rid of, is the pomp of the progress of royalty, but if he did how the English would hate him ! For your Englishman loves a procession, he loves the flare of colours and the beat of drums, he loves the procession which leads up to a gorgeous climax, the symbol of brave deeds, the symbol of what is meant by a royal leader. But Mr. Leacock evidently thinks that our pomp is a sham, in Canada they worship with the heart and do not need to show it by outward symbolism. It may be the better way but it will not do over here.

" As for taking him over to the Y.M.C.A. to play pin pool they never think of it. They have seen so much of the mere outside of his kingship that they don't understand the heart of it as we do in Canada."

Leaving the monarchy, and I suggest that Mr.
Leacock is genuinely serious about it, we shall find
him seriously humourous about the House of
Commons.

Mr. Leacock admits that it is an " interesting "
body. Of course it is the mission of Mr. Leacock
to be funny and he is to a certain extent funny
about the House of Commons. But he is sometimes
more than funny, he is merely superficial! I quote
here a few lines from Mr. Leacock in which he
more or less says that the House of Commons does
nothing. I am quite aware that Mr. Leacock is
clever enough to be able to write humourous books
but I do not think that he is clever enough to make
fun of the House of Commons without making
himself somewhat cheap.

" The House, however, is called together at very
frequent intervals to give it an opportunity of
hearing the latest legislation and allowing the
members to indulge in cheers, sighs, groans, votes and
other expressions of vitality. After having cheered
as much as is good for it, it goes back again to the
lunch rooms and goes on eating till needed again."

This sort of thing merely reads like some kind of
anarchistic journal desiring the suppression of the
Commons. It is quite unworthy of such a clever
humourist as Mr. Leacock.

But a little further on, when under the guise of
satire, Mr. Leacock is serious again, he manages to
say a very telling thing. The few lines I quote,
could, if necessary, open up a frightful controversy
about the Power of the Press.

" One of the leading neswpaper proprietors of London himself told me he has always felt that if he had the House of Commons on his side he had a very valuable ally."

It is in these days rather unfortunate for the House of Commons if it fails to ally itself with the big daily journals and it pays the House to be an ally of some of the great proprietors who have turned journalism into a vicious menace or a supreme good, as they choose.

Mr. Leacock says at least one thing about the House of Commons that is amusing and it is about the Speaker. This time the humour is of a rich quality.

" Towards the close of the evening a member rose and asked the Government if they knew what time it was. The Speaker however, ruled this question out of order on the ground that it had been answered before."

The whole of Mr. Leacock's attitude to the House of Commons is one of amused satire but unfortunately for the most part, it is not very amusing. It is as futile to attempt to be funny about the House of Commons as it is futile to try and shake the Capitol of Washington with little gibes. Mr. Leacock is amusing about London, he is amusing about the question addressed to the Spaker but in regard to the House of Commons he is laboured, his " wit " is very cheap. Here is quotation about the process of " scrapping." It is silly and almost childish.

" At the close of the play Lord Beatty who is

urbanity itself, offered to scrap Portsmouth Dockyard and asked if anybody present would like Canada."

The question of " scrapping " warships is not the kind of subject that lends itself to the pen of Mr. Leacock. In other words, the subject does not readily lend itself to burlesque and Mr. Leacock who uses this weapon pretty often, almost as much as observation, fails to " come off." I have an idea that Mr. Leacock would be far more effective if he treated the House of Commons with either extreme anger or extreme tolerance, as it is he sends at it, arrows or sarcasm but the arrows are blunt and fall with a hollow clang.

. . . .

Perhaps one of the most interesting parts of Mr. Leacock's book about England is that which deals with the British and American Press. Very concisely and accurately does Mr. Leacock state the difference in the two presses of the " presenting " of the news. In concerns the use of headlines, that question about which morality councils and other pernicious organisations rant with considerable frequency.

" This is where the greatest difference lies between the British newspapers and those of the United States and Canada. With us in America the great thing is to get the news and shout it at the reader ; in England they get the news and then break it to him as gently as possible. Hence the big headings, the bold type, and the double columns of the American paper, and the small headings and the general air of quiet and respectability of the English Press."

Mr. Leacock very wisely will not commit himself as to which method is the better. It is wise, for there are very fundamental differences in the functions that the two presses have to perform. And not the least perhaps is the question of size, not only of the newspapers themselves but of the area they have to cover. And not only says Mr. Leacock is there a difference in " presenting " there is also a great difference in the atmosphere, the way of looking at things, almost a question of values. Again Mr. Leacock deals with this position very clearly and also amusingly.

" In other words there is a difference of atmosphere. It is not merely the type and the lettering, it is a difference in the way the news is treated and the kind of words that are used. In America we love such words as " gun men " and " joy ride " and " death cell ' ; in England they prefer " person of doubtful character " and " motor travelling at excessive speed," and " corridor No. 6."

In a word, the American is more direct than us, he hits you in the eye with a wallop, he throws the story at you without any kind of apology, the newspaperman has printed the story for the public and the public has got to read it whether it likes it or not.

Once again another difference that Mr. Leacock points out. It is to do with the opening of the piece of news to be imbibed by the thirsty reader.

It is a pandering to the American "hustle," the perpetual energy that wants to get the most in the minimum of time.

"In the American paper the idea is that the reader is so busy that he must first be offered the news in one gulp. After that if he likes it he can go and eat some more of it. So the opening sentence must give the whole thing."

Mr. Leacock gives such an admirable example of the American direct method that I feel it well to reproduce it here.

"Seated in his room at the Grand Hotel with his carpet slippers on his feet and his body wrapped in a blue dressing gown with pink insertions, after writing a letter of farewell to his wife and emptying a bottle of Scotch whisky in which he exonerated her from all culpability in his death, Congressman Ahaseurus P. Tigg was found by night watchman, Henry T. Smith, while making his rounds as usual with four bullets in his stomach.'

This is certainly not picturesque but it gets the news over quickly.

And not only with the news does the American press deal sensationally, it also blazens out the smaller items. It is all very different to our sedateness over here. Again Mr. Leacock must be quoted.

"As with the world news so it is with the minor events of ordinary life--birth, death, marriage, accidents, crime. Let me give an illustration. Suppose that in a suburb of London a housemaid has endeavoured to poison her employer's family by putting a drug in the coffee. Now on our side of the water we should write that little incident up in a way to give it life, and put heading over it that would capture the reader's attention in a minue. We should begin it thus :

PRETTY PARLOR MAID
DEALS DEATH-DRINK
TO CLUBMAN'S FAMILY.

If we are too inquisitive and ask how the American pressmen know all these things Mr. Leacock gives the answer. I quote it, though as a matter of fact the real answer to the question as to how the American pressmen know so much is a very simple one, it is that they are American pressmen !

"The English reader would ask at once, how do we know that the parlour maid is pretty ? We don't. But out artistic sense tells us that she ought to be. Pretty parlour maids are the only ones we take any interest in : if an ugly parlour maid poisoned her employer's family we should hang her. Then, again the English reader would say how do we know that the man is a clubman ? Have we ascertained this fact definitely and if so, of what club or clubs is he a member ? Well, we don't know, except in so far as the thing is self-evident."

Mr. Leacock uses his powers of deduction, he knows well enough that a man is *not* poisoned by a pretty housemaid without some cause and also he knows only too well where the type of men to be poisoned by housemaids are most likely to be found.

" Any man who has romance enough in his life to be poisoned by a pretty housemaid ought to be in a club."

All this gets us back to the essential fact that though the American press is less dignified than the British press, it gets through to the apex of things at once. Wisely Mr. Leacock does not say which system of journalism he likes best. The moral is that there is a *difference* in the two presses and I think that Mr. Leacock believes that they had better remain different. And he is right, unity in some matters may be more of a curse than a blessing.

.   .   .   .

Mr. Leacock tells us that his main idea in coming to England was to find out if the English had any sense of humour. He must have come with the *a priori* assumption that they had, or surely he would not have come ! Really Mr. Leacock came to the conclusion that England and America were much the same in respect of appreciation of humour. From observation the professor came to the conclusion that " speaking by and large, the two communities are on the same level. A Harvard audience, as I have reason gratefully to acknowledge, is wonderful. But an Oxford audience is just as good." The academic audiences then are apparently the same. So also those who are not academic but commercial, they have an equal amount of stolidness.

" A gathering of business men in a textile town in the Midlands is just as heavy as a gathering of business men in Decatur, Indiana, but no heavier."

But yet there is one very vital difference between England and America in respect of lecture audiences. It is not so much a question of humour as a question of what is expected by the people gathered together. English audiences, Mr. Leacock thinks, want to be taught. He is supremely optimistic ! American audiences want to *see* a lecturer. Mr. Leacock is no doubt right about America, but English audiences like also to see people, of the people are worth seeing in the popular sense that they are somebody.

Mr. Leacock seems to have found English audiences somewhat dull. But I think it a mistake to think that they are dull, they are merely English ! The real difficulty he seems to have found was making an English audience *begin* to laugh, it takes them a long time to see anything. In this opinion I am sorry to say that Mr. Leacock is perfectly right in what he says. English audiences quite often are frightfully stolid, they seem quite incapable of appreciating anything that is at all subtle. Yet, this is so curious, you hardly ever find a joke fall flat in a music hall. Perhaps the English feel the solemnity of the lecture hall, at least the lecturer often does !

I am glad that Mr. Leacock pays a well merited compliment to the way in which the Scotch people respond to humour.

" There is, for a humourous lecturer, no better audience in the world than a Scottish audience.

The old standing joke about the Scotch sense of humour is mere nonsense. Yet one finds it everywhere."

Like every other lecturer who has existed from the time of the stone age, Mr. Leacock has been confronted with the type of person in the audience who appears to be a concrete statue, a model of silence, an epic of gloom, a monument of misery. Mr. Leacock finds him in all parts of the world, the man who has no sense of humour or is it that he has such an enormous understanding of humour that he cannot be expected to laugh at mere jokes at which more ordinary mortals guffaw merrily ?

" I find," writes Mr. Leacock, " for example, that wherever I go there is always seated in the audience, about three seats from the front, a silent man with a big motionless face like a melon. He is always there. I have seen that man in every town or city from Richmond, Indiana, to Bournemouth, in Hampshire. He haunts me. I get to expect him. I feel like nodding to him from the platform. What he thinks I don't know."

Let me give one final quotation from Mr. Leacock on the question of whether the English have any sense of humour.

" One final judgment, however, might with due caution be hazarded. I do not think on the whole, the English are quite as fond of humour as we are. I mean they are not so willing to welcome at all times the humorous point of view as we are in America."

.   .   .   .

I suggest that the humour of Mr. Leacock is really derived from two sources, observation and satire. It stands to reason therefore that he cannot expect to always " come off." I have shown how in my opinion, his satire of the House of Commons is somewhat weak for the very good reason that satire is of no avail against such an institution. Perhaps the humour of Mr. Leacock is at its best in his impressions of lecture audiences and his queer whimsical satire of the British and American Press methods. Mr. Leacock is nearly always good natured, even his satire has no trace of sneering. He has a terrific regard for America and he would quite evidently like us to share in that regard. And any Englishman who is not a fool cannot help doing so ; that wonderful spectacle of a terrific country across a terrific Ocean.

Mr. Leacock seems to think quite generally that we have a fair sense of humour but we take a longish time to get going. On the whole I think that he likes our little Island and he seems to like our audiences even if sometimes their sluggishness exasperates him somewhat.

Mr. Leacock set out to discover England and England has been glad to be " discovered " by Mr. Leacock. His many books have delighted many thousands of readers and his humour has sent ripples of laughter over nearly all the world. Given a congenial subject, his humour is certain and delicate, given an uncongenial subject, it is rather strained and laboured.

But behind all his humour there is a certain

kindliness towards mankind and mankind responding has a liking for the Professor from Canada.

END OF PEEP EIGHT.

Peep Number Nine.

ARNOLD BENNETT AND AN
EARLY BOOK.

WHEN a novelist achieves the fame that has come to Mr. Bennett, it is not without interest to get back and look at a very early book of such a writer. In this Essay there is one thing that I have no intention of attempting. I do not intend to attempt any comparson between the early and the late work of Mr. Bennett. Any such attempt in a short Essay such as the present would be abominably impertinent and quite useless. But what I shall endeavour to do, is to make some examination of " The Man from the North," and try and indicate to those who have forgotten or who have never known, what sort of novelist Mr. Bennett was in his early days. Those who wish to attempt a comparison of this book with one of his latest can easily do so for themselves. For my purpose it is sufficient that I should write something of the Mr. Bennett before he was world famous. Some who may read this Essay may not know what the story is, in " The Man from the North." Suffice it to say that it is the tale of a potential author, rather a

sad theme for the author remains more or less
potential.

.   .   .   .

" The Man from the North" is rather a sad
book for failure is sad and it is often even sadder
than success. And the failure of a would be
artist is the saddest thing in the world, the pictures
that are never printed, the books that are never
published, the songs that are never sung, the wild
dreams and the wild despairs, the alternating
hopes and fears, so sad it is, because it is so
inevitable. But I am anticipating. When the
book that Mr. Bennett wrote so many years ago
now, starts, it shows us a young man convinced
that he is going to succeed, for he is off to London,
that city where there are more devils and less
angels than anywhere in the whole wide world.
And let me hasten to add that I do not mean
human devils and human angels. I mean artistic
devils, that is the artistic failures, I mean artistic
angels, that is the artistic successes.

On the very first page of " The Man from the
North " Mr. Bennett tells what sort of man his
hero is, one Richard Larch. He is one of those
who see in London the goal of all ambitions,
listen, listen, quite quietly please, that sweet
sound is it not the bells of Bow Church, you bells
are you to be thoroughly trusted ?

This then is the sort of man that Richard
Larch is, he comes from the North Country,
that country towards which the great expresses

rush when they have left the dirty charm of Kings Cross far, far behind.

" There grows in the North Country a certain kind of youth of whom it may be said that he is born to be a Londoner. The metropolis and everything that appertains to it, that comes down from it, that goes up into it, has for him an imperious fascination, long before schooldays are over he learns to take a doleful pleasure in watching the exit of the London train from the railway station."

And why is this ? It is because London is the magnet, it can satisfy everything from sexual lust to patient endurance, it can make a millionaire and it can more easily drag a wasted life from the Thames, it can take a man and throw his name all around the world or it can take a man and lose him so that it would take the police several months to find him. For London never cares, it is eternal, it watches the birth pangs and says nothing it watches the death struggle in the enormous bedroom and the death struggle in the stinking garret and it sheds no tears, it is the home of a thousand religions, it is nearly as big as God but it thinks itself bigger and it defies Him with impunity.

" Sooner or later, perhaps by painful roads, he reaches the goal of his desire. London accepts him—on probation ; and as his strength is, so she demeans herself. Let him be bold and reso- lute, and she will make an obeisance, but her heel is all too ready to crush the coward and hesitant ;

and her victims, once underfoot, do not often rise again."

Well, let us go on some way when Richard has been some time in London, when he is trying to do something at journalism, when he is wishing for, and yet dreading more than anything in the world, the knock of the postman. Mr. Bennett describes the coming of the postman with a grim realism. Perhaps no one brings so much joy and sorrow as the postman yet he, delightful fellow that he is, walks calmly along the street and cares not what joy or what misery he pushes through our box.

" He remained at home in the evening, waiting for the last delivery, which was about 9.30. The double knocks of the postman were audible ten or twelve houses away. At last Richard heard him mounting the steps of No. 74, and then his curt rat tat shook the house. A little thud on the bare wooden floor of the hall seemed to indicate a heavier package than the ordinary letter."

But, alas and alas, it was was not anything very exciting, only a returned manuscript while outside London roared away in its callous merriment and melancholy.

But the coming back of the manuscript is one of those bitter disappointments that fill so many with a cruel despair. Poor Richard was reduced to reading the old rejection slip again and again. But, Mr. Bennett points out, the young author to be is not beaten as yet.

" He could not bring himself even to glance

through it, and finally it was sent to another magazine exactly as it stood."

It is the end of an episode but it is the beginning of a failure, a fall from the artistic to the commonplace, a fall from the hopes of high individual attainments to the growing conviction of a dead level. Mr. Bennett is tracing the progress of a man who is destined to be commonplace, merely one of a crowd, a pawn in the game.

With a grim realism, Mr. Bennett draws a picture of the dullness of Sunday in London.

He gives a very skilful picture of the difference in atmosphere between the Church of England with its religion and the Catholic Church with her religion.

" Richard's Sabbaths had become days of dismal torpor. A year ago, on first arriving in London, he had projected a series of visits to churches famous either for architectural beauty or for picturesque ritual. A few weeks however had brought tedium. He was fundamentally, irreligious, and his churchgoing proceeded from a craving, purely sensuous, which sought gratification in ceremonial pomps, twilight atmospheres heavy with incense and electric with devotion and dim perspectives of arching stone. But these things he soon discovered lost their fine savour by the mere presence of a prim congregation secure in the brass armour of self complacency ; for him the worship was spoilt by the worshippers."

Alas and alas, it is always so in the heathen

country that is called England, in the pagan city that is called London.

So unsatisfied, Richard goes to that Church,which is unpopular in England because it is so immeasurably superior to the national Church of the land.

"And so the time came when the only church which he cared to attend—and even to this he went but infrequently, lest use should stale its charm—was the Roman Catholic oratory of St. Philip Neri, where at Mass, the separation of the sexes struck a grateful note of austerity and the mean appearance of the people contrasted admirably with the splendour of the priests' vestments, the elaborate music and the gilt and colour of altars. Here deity was omnipotent and humanity abject."

The difference then, that humanity went to the Catholic Church because it really feared a God, while in the Church of England humanity is only afraid that it may fail to attain to the degree of smugness occasioned by that Church.

"Men and women of all grades, casting themselves down before the holy images in the ecstatic abandonment of repentance prayed side by side, oblivious of everything save their sins and the anger of a God. As a spectacle The Oratory was sublime."

.   .   .   .

Let me go on some way in the life of Richard Larch, he has arrived at a deathbed. Perhaps he wonders how the self complacent worshippers will look when they are on their death beds.

Mr. Bennett gives a really frightful picture of death by pneumonia, while outside, poor bloody fools, the careless population laughed and giggled —while—the angel of death giggled and watched and only waited.

" People were walking down the street ; they talked and laughed. How incongruously mirthful and careless their voices sounded."

While inside in a small room, it was the end of one man, the beginning of the great adventure, the great adventure that comes sooner or later to the nun or the prostitute, the saint or the diabolical murderer.

" Perhaps they had never watched by a sick bed, never listened to the agonised breathing of a pneumonia patient."

Good for them if they have not, the giggling lustful girls, the young man crazy for sex, their turn comes only too soon. It is good that they shall laugh and giggle, for they do not know that in the very little house they are passing, death is ready for a good square meal.

" That incessant intake of air ! It exasperated him. If it did not stop soon he should go mad. He stared at the gas flame, the gas flame grew larger, larger, till he could see nothing else. Then after a long time surely the breathing was more difficult ! There was a reverberating turmoil in the man's chest which shook the bed. Could Richard have been asleep or what ? He started up ; but Mr. Aked clung desperately to him, raising his shoulders higher and higher in the

struggle to inhale, and leaning forward till he was
bent almost double."

Mr. Bennett is not I think very fond of doctors,
he knows their callous " inhumanity " only too
well. He gives a fragment of the conversation
of these profesional men when they have discovered that the pneumonococcus has won.

" I tell you honestly," the doctor said, " I'm
so overworked that I should be quite satisfied to
step into my coffin and not wake again. I've had
three 3 a.m. midwifery cases this week—forceps,
chloroform and the whole bag of tricks—on the
top of all this influenza and I'm about sick of it.
That's the worst of our trade ; it comes in slumps.
What do you say, nurse ? "

In this Essay, I am merely attempting to show
something of the early work of Mr. Bennett,
pictures, as it were, of how he paints different
scenes in the life of Richard Larch. Poor Richard
Larch in his life of disappointed ambition, no
literary honours for him, no joy of seeing his name
hurled about North, South, East and West.
And even in love he is disappointed. The girl
he thinks he would have loved has gone to America.
Oh, the awful misery of the departure of the boat
train. And then when it has gone, what is there
to do, why, go back to London go back
to the genial feminine devils waiting for his
money and waiting for his soul, but even
London and all its painted women cannot destroy
his soul. But for the time he is done, the first
woman who comes will get him. Why, the

professional prostitute makes half her living from
the men who have either seen their sweethearts
leave by the boat train or heard that they have
thrown in their lot with some other man. And
a good thing too, the feminine devil who lurks
at the street corners may save from despair,
fornication may be one of the seven deadly sins,
but it saves from the sin against the Holy Ghost,
I mean, despair in those moments when the train
has gone or the coffin has gone. The resistance
of Richard is over for the time being. Mr. Bennett
puts the matter delicately and sympathetically.

" Looking down a side street, he saw a man
talking to a woman. He went past them and
heard what they said. Then he was in Shaftes-
bury Avenue. Curious sensations fluttered through
his frame. With an insignificant oath, he nerved
himself to resolve."

But it took him some time to make up his mind.
It takes a man some time to make up his mind
to indulge in promiscuity, all the traditions rise
up against him, his mother, the spotless " purity "
of his sisters,but sex always conquers at the time
and it beat poor Richard, for was not the boat
train hurtling his beloved one farther and farther
away every moment ?

" Would it end in his going quietly home ?
He crossed over into the seclusion of Whitcombe
Street to argue the matter. As he was passing
the entry to a court, a woman came out, and both
had to draw back to avoid a collision."

Defeat for the moment. Richard had joined

the vast majority of those men who do not wait
for the delicate virginity of their wives.

"*Cheri*," she murmured. She was no longer
young but her broad, Flemish face showed kindliness and good humour in every feature of it, and
her voice was soft. He did not answer, and she
spoke to him again. His spine assumed the
consistency of butter; a shuddering thrill ran
through him. She put her arm gently into his
and pressed it. He had no resistance."

The rejection slip, the self-complacent congregation and the departure of the boat train have
led to a logical climax, a hired woman just because
she is a woman. And, please note that, not
necessarily *lust*, you who are always moral and well
fed and comfortable and never in a city by yourself.

    .   .   .   .

Quite carefully, Mr. Bennett traces the gradual
failure of Larch in all his literary ambitions. It is
a sad story and paints life as a hard cruel thing.
He had even been forced to join an unpromising
literary society!

Really no doubt Mr. Bennett wishes us to know
that the reason why Larch failed was that he
had no real literary ability. He had ideas but
could not use them.

"At length an idea! He was not going to fail,
after all. The story must of course begin with a
quarrel between old Downs and his daughter.
He drew up to the table, took a pen, and wrote

the title ; then a few sentences hurriedly and then a page. Then read what was written, pronounced it unconvincing rubbish and tore it up. Words were untractable, and besides he could not see the scene. He left the table and after studying a tale of de Maupassant's, started on a new sheet, carefully imitating the manner of that writer. But he could by no means satisfy himself."

Which is an extremely probable reason why he could not satisfy anyone else. The whole thing is hopeless, Richard has no chance.

" The plot tumbled entirely to pieces ; the conclusion especially was undramatic ; but how to alter it ? "

Yet Richard is still not entirely without ambitions, his ideal dies hard, the death rattle of the literary ambition is long and tenacious, there was plenty of time."

" He could afford to wait—to wait till he had made a reputation and half a score of women elegant and refined were only too willing to envelop him in an atmosphere of adoration."

So very gradually Mr. Bennett leads us to the inevitable end, there has been the inevitable rejection slip, the inevitable street woman, the inevitable second and third attempt to write, and then the end ; I mean the end of an ambition and the beginning of a quite uneventful life that would go on and on. Mr. Bennett shows us the scene only too surely.

" He knew that he would make no further attempt to write. Laura was not even aware that he had ambitions in that direction. He had never told her, because she would not have understood. She worshipped him, he felt sure, and at times he had a great tenderness for her, but it would be impossible to write in the suburban doll's house which was to be their's. No! In future he would be simply the suburban husband —dutiful towards his employers, upon whose grace he would be doubly dependent ; keeping his house in repair, pottering in the garden ; taking his wife out for a walk or occasionally to the theatre ; and saving as much as he could. He would be good to his wife—she was his."

And yet even then his literary ambition would not be entirely eclipsed. It would be in the future, he would not himself produce a book, but something that he might produce, might in the time to come produce a work of literary art.

" Perhaps a child of his might give a sign of literary ability. If so—and surely these instincts descended, were not lost—how he would foster and encourage it."

Thus Mr. Bennett does not leave us with the black tragedy, in the dim distance shines a star of hope and it is something that has to do with the most wonderful thing in all the world ; a little child.

END OF PEEP NINE,

THE END.